Corporate Crime
Corporate Violence
A Primer

Corporate Crime
Corporate Violence
A Primer

Nancy K. Frank
University of Wisconsin—Milwaukee

Michael J. Lynch
Florida State University—Tallahassee

Harrow and Heston
PUBLISHERS
New York

Harrow and Heston, Publishers
Stuyvesant Plaza
P.O. Box 3934
Albany, N.Y. 12203

Library of Congress CIP:

Frank, Nancy.
     Corporate crime, corporate violence : a primer / Nancy K. Frank, Michael J. Lynch. — Rev. and expanded ed.
        P. cm. — (A Harrow and Heston special edge supplementary text)
     Rev. ed. of: Crimes against health and safety / Nancy Frank.
     Includes bibliographical references and index.
     ISBN 0-911577-23-8 : $15.50
        1. Commercial crimes—United States. 2. Consumer protection—Law and legislation—United States—Criminal provisions. 3. Industrial safety—Law and legisla-tion—United States—Criminal provisions. 4. Offenses against the environment—United States. 5. Corporations—United States—Corrupt practices.   I. Lynch, Michael J. II. Frank, Nancy. Crimes against health and safety.
III. Title.
KF9350.F7 1992
345.73'0242—dc2O
[347.3052421]   92–25071
                                                 CIP

This book is a revised and expanded edition of *Crimes Against Health and Safety* by Nancy K. Frank, first published in 1985: original L.C. Number: 85-081734, original ISBN: 0-911577-05-X,

Contents

About the Authors

Michael J. Lynch is an Associate Professor, Program in Criminal Justice at Florida State University's School of Criminology and Criminal Justice. He received his Ph.D. from the State University of New York at Albany in 1988. His publications include *A Primer in Radical Criminology* with W. Byron Groves, and *Race and Criminal Justice* with E. Britt Patterson. His interests include theories of crime, corporate and white-collar crime, punishment, and radical criminology.

Nancy Frank received her doctoral degree in criminal justice from the School of Criminal Justice at the State University of New York at Albany and is an Associate Professor at the University of Wisconsin—Milwaukee. She received a Distinguished Dissertation Award for her work on the development of civil and criminal sanctions for health and safety violations. Her works include several books and a number of articles concerning corporate crime and the regulation of health and safety problems. Currently, she is interested in the social control of technological risk during the late twentieth century.

One

Quiet Violence

DEADLY POLLUTANTS, emitted by the manufacturing sector
of the economy, cause increased rates of cancer among the
general population, dramatically increase the rate of birth
defects among new-born infants (Utne Reader 1990) and kill
people, the environment and wildlife (Luoma 1991). At work,
people receive crippling injuries or are exposed to unsafe
workplace environments, including deadly chemicals, lethal
machinery, and air laced with toxic, carcinogenic contaminants
(Simon and Eitzen 1990; Swartz 1975). Gruesome animal experimentation inflicts great pain and torturous deaths upon countless laboratory creatures in order to produce consumer products that remain unsafe (Goodall 1989; American Anti-
Vivesection Society 1989; Kaufman 1989). Consumers are injured and killed by knowingly faulty and dangerous consumer
goods. Unnecessary and dangerous nuclear waste, radiation
and chemical pollution are produced by the corporate sector

("chemical crimes of industry," Simon and Eitzen 1990, 6). The world's pristine forests and jungles are being exhausted to provide appealing packaging for consumer products in our throw-away society (Connelly 1991; Mardon 1991; DeBonis 1991). Agricultural, migrant and third world workers are poisoned through the use of unnecessary pesticides on large corporate farms and plantations (Weir and Shapiro 1982). All these are examples of the types of quiet corporate violence that people throughout the world experience each and every day of their lives.

Typically, people do not conceptualize such acts as violence or as crimes. Most often, these acts are viewed as unfortunate but unavoidable accidents associated with a technologically oriented society (see: Lynch *et al.* 1989; and chapter 9). When workers are injured or killed, we tend to blame the workers (the victims) rather than the unsafe work conditions established by employers. When industry pollutes the environment, tests products on animals, or clear cuts forests and drives species into extinction, we view these acts as the cost of progress. This commonly accepted view of corporate activities hides the violent nature of these acts. Yet, many argue that the forms of social harm reviewed above are as serious or even more serious than the types of interpersonal violence our society treats as crime (Sutherland 1949; Michalowski 1985; Quinney 1979; Reiman 1990; Lynch and Groves 1989). This argument is hinged upon three claims.

First, we fail to view dangerous corporate behaviors as violence because they violate the visual image of violence we store in our heads—an image that is reinforced each and every day by the media and the activities of law enforcement agencies. This image depicts crime as a one-on-one harm (Reiman 1990,50), committed by young, lower class, urban males who also tend to be minorities (Reiman 1990, 40-46). Consequently, when we are presented with violent acts that do not fit our preconceived picture of violent crime, we do not respond to the act as a violent act. In other words, where harms are indirect, where violence is accomplished without traditionally recognized weapons (e.g., with consumer products rather than guns and knives), where organizations rather than individuals are the responsible actors, when powerful, upper class persons are the offenders, we seem to be unwilling to label the act as serious violence.

Second, our images of crime and law enforcement activities, reinforced by the media, lead us to believe that the most serious form of crime in society (i.e., the most dangerous and the type we are most likely to be victimized by) is common street crime or ordinary crime (Reiman 1990). This is not the case, however. People are much more likely to be victimized by silent, corporate violence than by ordinary street crimes (Box 1984; Michalowski 1985; Messerschmidt 1986; Reiman 1990).

Third and finally, the reason we fail to treat corporate violence as a crime relates to the power of corporate actors and their ability to influence the scope, content and focus of law (Michalowski 1985; Simon and Eitzen 1990; Messerschmidt 1986; Box 1983; Chambliss and Seidman 1982). We will discuss this problem more fully in chapter 3. For now, it is sufficient to note that law enforcement and media attention are not likely to be directed toward the types of violent crimes the powerful commit.

Whether our society treats corporate violence as crimes or ignores these acts, the fact remains that corporations and the consumer society of which they are a part, produce hazardous products, workplace conditions, and environmental waste and destruction that threaten the lives, health and safety of a large segment of the population.

The alarming extent of corporate violence world-wide has a great deal to do with run-away technology, and our societal belief that science and technology produce social progress. Within a relatively unregulated free market economy (nationally and internationally) economic pressures exerted upon corporations require the production of ever more, new and appealing products for an ever greater number of people. This has led corporations to rely more heavily upon technology and science to produce unique products at a faster and faster pace. This reliance on science and technology has produced a higher standard of living and a greater number of choices for consumers. Seldom, however, are the costs of this economic freedom acknowledged (see chapter 9). These costs include increased pain, violence and death for people, animal life, and the environment. As a society, we appear to have developed a mass-corporate cost-benefit consciousness that overlooks individual pain and suffering if a greater good, calculated monetarily, can be achieved (e.g., see the Ford Pinto case discussed in chapter 4; see also chapter 9).

To claim that corporations are responsible for creating a great deal of violence does not imply that corporate executives are callous, uncaring or immoral individuals. Some truly believe that they are involved in a struggle to create a better world. They do not *want* to see people killed or the environment destroyed, but they *accept* some amount of death and destruction as inevitable in order to make the world better for the rest of us. Their view is reinforced by the very structure of modern society, by factors (e.g. political, economic and legal) that impinge upon, create, direct and allow death and destruction—violence—to be viewed as an inevitable cost of modernization. In short, corporate executives cannot bear all the blame: the entire structural context of modern society—its economic system, political organization and leadership, social organization and expectations, and legal system—contribute in some way to the commission of corporate crimes of violence.

Increased Concern over Corporate Crime and Violence

Over the past two decades, a number of tragic episodes have elevated public consciousness concerning the quiet forms of corporate violence briefly reviewed above (Cullen *et al.* 1987, 1984, 1982; Katz 1980). The Love Canal disaster, in which an entire neighborhood was evacuated because it had been built on an abandoned chemical dump, became the prelude to a growing awareness of hazardous waste disposal problems and the quiet, hidden and acceptable ways in which corporations prey upon consumers, workers, the general public, and even the environment. In the Love Canal case, Hooker Chemical Company disposed of some 40 million pounds of toxic chemicals in a landfill over an eleven year time period, and later sold the landfill to a local board of education for $1 (Simon and Eitzen

1990, 6; Brown 1980). As Simon and Eitzen (1990, 6) note, Love Canal is "the tip of the United States' waste iceberg...90 percent of the United States' waste is illegally disposed of." For instance, there are currently more than 21,000 known hazardous waste sites in the U.S. These sites cause serious illness and death by polluting drinking water supplies in over 15,000 American communities.

Another case that added to public concern over corporate violence was the Ford Pinto case (Cullen *et al.* 1987, 1984), in which the Ford Motor Company was indicted on charges of reckless homicide for intentionally selling Pintos that tended to explode in rear-end collisions (see chapter 4). In addition, the accident at Three Mile Island, in which the core of a nuclear reactor began to melt down before technicians were able to bring it under control, vividly illustrated the risks that are *created* and *managed* by profit-seeking firms. Even more dramatic events abroad, such as the nuclear disaster at Chernobyl in the Soviet Union and the escape of deadly poisonous gases at Union Carbide plants in Bhopal, India, which caused thousands of deaths and injuries (Lynch *et al.* 1989; Weir 1987), caused many Americans to wonder whether similar incidents were "waiting to happen" in their own backyards.

More recently, concern over the "green-house effect" and its link to deforestation in the U.S., Canada (Connelly 1991), South America, Malaysia and other Asian countries (Mardon 1991), as well as the medical waste disaster that plagued east coast beaches during the summers of 1988 and 1989 (Simon and Eitzen 1990, 8), continue to expose unsound corporate practices that create violence.

Along with these dramatic episodes has come an increasing awareness and concern about the risks that surround us in our daily lives. Hardly a day goes by without our hearing some news story about a newly identified risk. A food additive is suspected of causing cancer. A drug is suspected of causing birth defects. We are warned of the dangers of radiation emanating from our color televisions and our computer monitors. Studies have connected automobile exhaust to respiratory illness. Experts argue that automobile pollution, along with industrial pollution (CFCs in particular), are eating away at the ozone layer, increasing the likelihood of skin cancer, and contributing to the "green house effect" (Barry 1991). So much bad news comes to us about such risks that many people begin to question the experts, and to deny that these dangers even exist.

Many of the most severe problems that face the world today—pollution, rain forest depletion, exploding landfills, energy crises, unsafe products and working conditions, etc. — have been blamed on consumer excesses and demands. However, the behavior of consumers (like the behavior of corporations and corporate executives) is itself the product of modern social and economic forces (Sale 1990). The causes of many of the threats to our safety, health, and the environment are extremely complex. Pollution, rain forest depletion, exploding landfills, the energy crisis, and other concerns cannot be explained by simple notions of greed and immorality. Instead, an understanding of these problems requires us to recognize that the behavior of consumers, farmers in the Third World, or multinational corporations is, in each case, a product of modern social and economic forces. The logic of these forces puts pressure on producers to cut costs and develop new products that will appeal to consumers. For example, when fast food chains started using Styrofoam hamburger boxes instead of paper wrappers or cardboard, the motivation was to cut costs by increasing the shelf-life of fast foods and appealing to consumers by delivering the food hotter than before. Consumers liked the new containers because they were able to take food out and have it stay hot until they were ready to eat it. No one wanted to destroy the ozone layer around the earth (a by-product of Styrofoam production) and, as a result, increase the incidence of skin cancer. But the chloroflourocarbons used to make Styrofoam, are strongly suspected of doing just that. Who is to blame for the increased cancer deaths a shift to Styrofoam containers may have caused? Consumers? Corporations?

Our goal in exploring the problems of corporate violence throughout this book is two-fold. First, we will describe the social and economic forces that generate corporate violence. Second, we will explore different levels of blameworthiness in the examples discussed throughout this book.

The Extent of Corporate Violence: A Brief Overview

While the public tries to take refuge in the hope that the greenhouse effect or cancer risks, or the other problems referred to above are greatly exaggerated, statistics coldly document the harms that surround us every day. Mining accidents claim the lives of 150 people annually, and injure another 50,000 (Department of Labor 1986). If all of these injuries and deaths were due to true accidents, we might be less concerned with them. But many occur because corporations show a blatant disregard for workers, and fail to comply with health and safety regulations that have been created to prevent these types of injury (e.g., Wallace 1987). One such accident, which killed 15 miners, occurred in a mine that "received 1,133 citations and fifty-seven orders for immediate correction of known dangers by federal inspectors" (Simon and Eitzen 1990, 136) in the previous three year period. Yet, the owners of the mine did not respond to the citations or orders, choosing instead to do nothing.

Each year occupational diseases cause 350,000 new illnesses, and between 50,000 and 70,000 workers die from occupational diseases (congressional testimony of Dr. Phillip Landrigan, cited in Corporate Crime Reporter 1988a:3. This estimate is conservative compared to the 100,000 to 200,000 occupational deaths estimated by others, see: Simon and Eitzen 1990:37-38). Researchers estimate that "corporate violence" kills and injures more people each year than all street crime combined (Reiman 1990, 57-64; Lynch and Groves 1989, 34-39; Michalowski 1985; Messerschmidt 1986). Michalowski (1985, 325), for example, notes that work related deaths are *six times* more likely than homicide, while Messerschmidt (1986, 99-100) and Reiman (1990, 61) conclude that a person is more likely to die trying to earn a living than at the hands of a common criminal.

Other statistics document how corporate crimes of violence reach us even where we think we are the safest: in the home. The Consumer Product Safety Commission (1983), for example, estimates that 28,000 deaths each year result from using consumer products (for discussion see Simon and Eitzen 1990, 117-118). In all, some 20 million Americans are injured in their homes; 110,000 of these people receive permanent or crippling injuries (Simon and Eitzen 1990, 117). Not counted in these estimates are the millions of people injured by unsafe consumer products shipped abroad (Weir and Shapiro 1980; Scanlan 1991; Michalowski 1985, 339-340).

Yet these statistics cannot begin to convey the *personal pain* of the victims and the circumstances that led to these quiet acts of violence. To illustrate these pains and circumstances, we turn to several case studies that examine the effects of corporate violence.

Case Studies of Corporate Violence

In 1975 a sixty-eight year-old woman died of pancreatic cancer. The following year, her husband died of cancer, and her forty-five year-old son developed leukemia. They had lived in Little Elk Valley near Elkton, Maryland, a quiet, rural community. The water and air in the valley was polluted with high concentrations of benzene, carbon tetrachloride, toluene, methyl-ethyl-ketone, and other dangerous chemicals. These chemicals were also found in blood samples of the valley's residents. At the bottom of the valley sat a small local business, the Galaxy Chemical Company which reclaimed waste solvents. Reports from plant workers and others indicated that chemicals from the plant were spilled and leaked into Little Elk Creek, contaminating local drinking water supplies (Brown 1980, 204-221).

During the late 1950s, a lab technician, Beulah Jordan, who was conducting tests of a new drug, MER/29, reported to her supervisor that one of the laboratory monkeys which had been given the drug was showing loss of weight and was apparently partially blind. According to congressional testimony, her superiors:

> ...then decided to throw out the sick male drug
> monkey...from the experiment and substitute another
> control monkey in his place which had never been on MER/
> 29. After this decision, Dr. van Maanen [director of

biological sciences for Merrell-Richardson, the manufacturer of MER/29] called Mrs. Jordan into his office and instructed her to make this substitution in working up the weight charts...Mrs. Jordan resented being asked to...render a false report, and refused to sign her charts. Dr. King [her supervisor] ordered her never to mention the substitution. She was told that this was the way the company wanted it and to forget it. She was told that this order had come from higher up and there was nothing she could do about it but obey the order and do as the "higher-ups" wanted.

MER/29 was approved by the FDA in May 1960 and marketed by Merrell-Richardson for almost two years, when the company withdrew the drug from the market. During those two years, doctors prescribing the drug to their patients reported baldness, skin damage, changes in reproductive organs, and eye cataracts in patients using the drug. Hundreds of thousands of people used the drug before it was finally withdrawn. A subsequent investigation of company records disclosed that before the drug was approved by the FDA, the company was aware of these side effects but failed to report them to the FDA (Silverman and Lee 1974, 89-93; Silverman *et al.*, 1982).

In 1969 an elderly woman was killed when the accelerator on her car locked at 25 miles per hour. The rubber motor mounts holding the car's engine in place had broken, causing the engine to lunge out of place, jamming the accelerator. From 1965-1969, General Motors Corporation sold 6.7 million Chevrolets with these rubber motor mounts. As early as 1965, the Pontiac division of General Motors had found these rubber mounts to be defective and substituted a safer mounting system. Although the Pontiac engineers passed along their findings to other GM divisions, Chevrolet continued to use the rubber mounts. In 1966, reports that mounts were breaking, causing accidents, injuries, and even deaths began to emerge. General Motors refused to recall the cars until 1971, when pressure from the government, consumer groups, and the news media could no longer be ignored. The recall cost the company $40 million dollars, at a time when it spent $200 million a year on advertising (DeLorean 1980, 43-45). This is not an isolated incident for G.M., whose Corvair was attacked by consumer advocate Ralph Nader (1965). In the 1980s, G.M. also had serious problems with its X-car line (the basic chassis design for four different G.M. cars) that were connected to 15 deaths (Simon and Eitzen 1990,120).

A common reaction to stories such as these is to ask: How could this happen? How could executives at Chevrolet continue to build cars when they were aware that design defects in the cars would cause accidents, and possibly injury and death? How could managers of the Galaxy Chemical Company ignore the plague of chemicals they were spewing into their own back-yard? How could executives at Merrell-Richardson falsify drug test results, ignoring the evidence that the drug they were selling to people could cause illness and even blindness? With our sense of incredulity also comes a sense of outrage at the utter irresponsibility that is reflected in these incidents.

One common reaction is to search for solutions to these problems, to find ways of preventing similar incidents from occurring in the future, and to provide some mechanism for punishing the irresponsibility that leads to such tragedies. One "solution" has been the creation of health and safety laws. Few areas of law have grown as quickly as health and safety law. During the late 1960s and through the 1970s, major legislation was passed relating to consumer health and safety, occupa-tional health and safety, and environmental health. These laws frequently created new crimes relating to conduct affecting health and safety and a new class of criminals, primarily business corporations and executives, who would be held responsible for breaches of these new laws. In other instances, traditional criminal laws were applied to punish persons who ignored health and safety concerns and who created intolerable risks of harm.

Two central issues must be examined with respect to these developments in the law:

1. Are they effective? That is, do these new laws and new applications of old laws provide effective solutions to

health and safety problems, offering greater protection than alternative solutions?

2. Are they fair? Do these laws apply the criminal sanction in ways that are consistent with our traditional notions of fairness in the criminal justice system? Are only the blameworthy punished? Are these acts so morally reprehensible that they merit criminal punishment?

Some years ago, a number of criminologists turned their attention from studying crime in the streets to a study of "crime in the suites." A considerable amount of work has been done in recent years on the subject of corporate and white-collar crime. The difficulty in studying corporate and white-collar crime, however, is that these categories include widely differing behaviors, many of which are morally neutral, such as violations of economic regulations (Kadish, 1963). Distinctly different are those actions of corporations and corporate officials which cause definite, physical harm to consumers, workers, the public and the environment.

This book examines corporate crimes of violence by identifying the legal issues that arise in regard to a number of specific examples of such crimes, especially those involving worker health and safety. We will also take a brief look at the causes of corporate crimes of violence and the problems encountered in attempting to control and prosecute these crimes, and raise the question of how the legal system can and ought to structure risks in order to lessen the amount of corporate violence that occurs in our society. Before examining these issues further, however, we need to examine what we mean by the terms "corporate crime" and "corporate violence."

Two

Corporate Crime: Definition and History

THE CONCEPTS OF corporate crime and corporate violence are of relatively recent origin. In this chapter, we spell out what we mean by the term corporate crime, and trace the development of this term. Provisionally, we can define corporate crimes as harmful acts committed by powerful organizations and the persons that occupy positions of importance within corporations. A more complete and precise definition of this term will emerge as we review the history of research in this area. We caution readers that the term corporate crime is often used synonymously with other terms such as "white-collar crime" or "organizational crime" or "elite deviance." Where appropriate, we will introduce and define each of these terms.

The Muckrakers: Corporate Crime in Popular Media

Widespread interest in the harmful activities of the "social elite" emerged during the early 1900s, when many of the excesses of America's corporate leaders like John D. Rockefeller,

Andrew Carnegie, Cornelius Vanderbilt and J. P. Morgan were exposed in the popular media by a group of writers known as the "muckrakers." Included in this group were well-known novelists, non-fiction writers and social historians such as Ida Tarbell, Lincoln Steffens, Sinclair Lewis, Upton Sinclair, and Charles Russell.

The muckrakers' targets—Rockefeller and his cohorts—were American heroes who captured the spirit of the American dream as well as the imagination of the American public. Many rose from poverty to power and fortune between the Civil War and 1900 (Josephson 1934, 32-44). These individuals played "the leading role in an age of industrial revolution," and sought "[t]o organize and exploit the resources of a nation upon a gigantic scale...in the name of an uncontrolled appetite for private profit...." (Josephson 1934, vii-viii). There were many parallels in the lives of these early industrialists: each was exposed to piety, prudence and shrewd business practices at an early age. Rockefeller's father, for instance, was said to "cheat his boys" and "skin'em" in trades at every opportunity in order to "make'em sharp" (Josephson 1934, 46). At a young age, Rockefeller used his father's lessons to engage in practices such as loan-sharking, which yielded a better rate of return than legal loans (Josephson 1934, 47). According to Ida Tarbell, Rockefeller never smiled or laughed except when he got the better of someone in a business deal (cited in Josephson 1934, 48-49). This was the type of unscrupulous character and personality trait that the muckrakers exposed to the general public. (For further examples related to others named above see: Josephson 1934, 50-74, 100-148, 253-289, 315-374).

However, the muckrakers' concerns went beyond the traits of the individuals who amassed great fortunes during America's Industrial Revolution. The muckrakers recognized the deeds of these individuals and their personalities as products of economic forces (Josephson 1934, viii). In the muckrakers' view, big business itself was to be condemned: big business was "bad business" insofar as it was more concerned with profit than human life (see Cullen *et al.* 1987, 46-47; Geis and Meier 1977, 5-7). The argument went further, and claimed that the powerful were corrupted by capitalism's drive to produce goods for less. Here, again, the behavior of the powerful was seen as affected by forces outside the individual: namely, large-scale, industrial capitalism drove capitalists to exploit workers and consumers.

Early Academic Interest in Corporate Crime

At about the same time that the muckrakers began to investigate early forms of corporate crime, similar claims were espoused by a sociologist, E.A. Ross. Ross's (1907[1977]) article on the "criminaloid" was the "first significant sociological statement about white-collar crime..." (Geis and Meier 1977, 7). In Ross' view, the criminaloid—the powerful and wealthy corporate and business leaders who victimized an unsuspecting public—enjoyed immunity from the law (Ross 1977, 20), exhibited a "moral insensibility" (p.31), "preferred to prey on the anonymous public" (p.31), and would continue to "flourish until the growth of morality overtakes the growth of opportunity to prey" (p.36). Given this view of the powerful criminaloid, it can be argued that Ross was waging a moral crusade against the excesses of the powerful in order to raise public consciousness and curb the harmful behavior of the powerful (Cullen et al 1987, 48). However, like the muckrakers' view of the powerful business elite, Ross' view also emphasized the influence of impersonal structural forces on the behavior of the powerful. Ross argued that the economic, social and moral context and climate of late 19th and early 20th century American society created the opportunity for the crimes of the criminaloid. The rub, however, was that many of the behaviors Ross analyzed were not defined as crimes by law—they were, and many continue to be, acceptable forms of business practice. Ross recognized this distinction between "moral" or "normative" and legal definitions of criminal behavior (see chapter 3), and employed the term "criminaloid" to emphasize the fact that he was concerned with behaviors that were not necessarily violations of existing criminal law. Ross nevertheless believed that many of the harms created by the powerful should be treated criminally, and argued that the same behaviors would be treated criminally if committed by the poor and powerless.

Aside from occasional exposés by scholars like Thorstein Veblen and Charles Beard, and consumer advocates such as Kallet and Schlink (1933), which continued to reveal the unsavory side of business practices, Ross' work on the criminaloid went virtually unnoticed for thirty years. Academics' attitudes toward the powerful and their misdeeds changed in the 1940s, however, largely due to the efforts of Edwin H. Sutherland.

Corporate Crime: A Maturing Idea

Sutherland (1940, 1941, 1945, 1949) was the first to set forth a full-blown theoretical perspective on white-collar crime. Unlike Ross or the muckrakers, Sutherland attempted to remain neutral to the crimes committed by America's business elite; he did not attempt to judge these crimes from a moralistic perspective, nor did he attempt to engineer a moral crusade against these harmful behaviors (Geis and Meier 1977, 7; Cullen *et al.* 1987, 48). Rather, he examined behaviors of the powerful which violated some form of law (criminal, administrative, or civil), society's reaction to these violations of law, and the reasons the upper class business person violated the law.

Sutherland's interest in white-collar crimes came about as the result of his interest in creating a general theory of criminal behavior that would explain all crime (i.e., his theory of differential association which claimed that criminal behavior is learned in small group interactions and involves excessive exposure to definitions that favor violation of the law, see Vold and Bernard 1986, 209-214, 225-229). Sutherland believed that existing theories of crime contained a class bias, and were inefficient because they could only explain why the poor committed crime (Sutherland 1983, 3-8). Sutherland argued that poverty could hardly explain why the rich and powerful violated the law (Sutherland 1983, 7; 1940, 1, 10). Thus, to fully explain all crime, a new theory was needed.

Sutherland labelled all violations of law by the powerful "white-collar crime," in an attempt to "bring it within the scope of criminology" (Sutherland 1940, 5). Sutherland defined white collar crime "as a crime committed by a person of respectability and high social status in the course of his occupation"

(Sutherland 1983, 7). This definition was used to exclude from his study ordinary crimes, such as "murder, intoxication or adultery" that the upper class person might commit *outside* of their *occupational roles* (Sutherland 1983, 7).

While Sutherland's work sensitized criminologists to the need to examine the crimes of the powerful, it was also responsible for several major debates over the meaning of the terms white-collar and corporate crime (e.g., Tappan 1947; Clinard and Quinney 1973; Hirschi and Gottfredson 1987; for a review of these issues see Kramer 1984). Two issues are of concern to us. The first centers on the observation that Sutherland's definition is ambiguous because it failed to define exactly what is meant by terms like "high social status" (Geis and Meier 1977, 253-254). This oversight has led some to argue that "farmers, repairmen and others in...non-white-collar occupations could...be classified as white collar violators" (Newman 1977, 52). This definitional uncertainty has recently led some (Hirschi and Gottfredson 1987, 1989) to suggest that this term has become so meaningless that it should be eliminated. We do not believe that this is the case. The term "upper social status" certainly does contain a certain amount of ambiguity, but not enough to classify T.V. repair-persons or farmers as white-collar offenders. This term is important because it emphasizes the fact that people who commit white-collar crimes are capable of doing so through the prestigious occupational positions they occupy. In other words, persons who hold white-collar jobs have the opportunity to commit specific types of crimes that people in non-white-collar position are denied.

Our second concern is with the conceptual confusion that has emerged in this area concerning the differences between white-collar and corporate crime. This problem, as Kramer (1984) and Clinard and Yeager (1980) note, can be traced to Sutherland's book, *White-Collar Crime* (1949). In this book, Sutherland employed the definition of white-collar crime cited above, yet examined violations of law by the 70 largest American manufacturing, mining and mercantile corporations over a 45 year time span (Sutherland 1983, 13). Thus, Sutherland did not examine the criminal behavior committed by *individuals* of respectability and high social status in the course of their occupation, he studied the illegal behavior of corporate entities. After years of debate, this conceptual confusion was clarified, and eventually led to the idea that white collar crimes and corporate crimes were separate and distinct acts (Clinard and Quinney 1973). We will employ this distinction throughout the remainder of this book.

To summarize the material we have reviewed above, let us set forth some specific definitions concerning white-collar and corporate crime. In our view, **white collar crimes** are: *socially injurious and blameworthy acts committed by individuals or groups of individuals who occupy decision-making positions in corporations and businesses, and which are committed for their own personal gain against the businesses and corporations that employ them.*

When we use the term **corporate crime**, we mean: *socially injurious and blameworthy acts, legal or illegal, that cause financial, physical or environmental harm, committed by corporations and businesses against their workers, the general public, the environment, other corporations and businesses, the government, or other countries. The benefactor of such crimes is the corporation.*

Corporate violence, then, *is a subset of all corporate crimes which includes:corporate crimes, as defined above, that cause physical injury to workers, the general public (both in the U.S. and abroad), or the environment (including land, air, water,animals and plants).*

The main features of the last definition are that the behavior must be (1) socially injurious, (2) blameworthy, (3) cause physical harm, (4) be committed by corporations and (5) that the act is meant to benefit the corporation as a whole, rather than specific individuals within the corporation.

Thus far, we have defined what we mean by corporate crime and violence, and have provided a few examples and case studies that illustrate the type of harm and extent of harm these crimes create. Before continuing our analysis of these problems, in the next chapter we turn to an examination of the process of defining these acts of violence as crimes.

Three

Calling a Crime a Crime

THE LEGAL DEFINITION of corporate "crime" is important for several reasons. First, it defines the widely recognized and institutionalized moral boundaries of acceptable conduct for corporations. Second, the law establishes a legal mechanism for punishing those who transgress moral boundaries. And third, law creates a system designed to deter corporate criminals. However, any definition of a corporate crime is likely to be problematic. Among the issues that arise are:

1. Whether corporate crimes create a just and fair system of liability in which only those who are morally blameworthy for the defined harms are punished.

2. Whether corporate crimes are defined in ways that actually protect the public, consumers, the work force or the environment.

This chapter will examine issues concerning the fairness and effectiveness of corporate crime laws, and will present theories for understanding how existing laws, imperfect as they may be, have come to pass.

Defining Rights and Responsibilities

Law is a the product of a political process used to define the rights and responsibilities of people in society. There are a number of different types of laws that political systems can devise. In this chapter we examine a variety of health and safety laws that are applied to corporate crimes of violence, including administrative law or regulatory law, civil law, and criminal law (see Meier 1985).

Regardless of which type of law is used, health and safety laws establish certain rights regarding how much we may expect to be protected from particular kinds of hazards to our health and safety, at work and as consumers. When a law creates a right for one class of persons, it necessarily establishes a responsibility for others. For example, the federal Occupational Safety and Health Act of 1970 established the rights of workers to a safe and healthful work environment. It also established a corresponding duty for employers to provide a place of employment that is free from recognized hazards.

Conventional criminal laws, such as those prohibiting theft or assault, specify rights and responsibilities recognized since ancient times and, consequently, are rarely the subject of serious disputes. Conversely, the responsibilities established in health and safety laws, and other laws which define corporate crimes, are relatively new and thus open for debate. Rapid technological developments create a constantly changing pool of economic opportunities and potential hazards. While various legal and ethical principles are relied upon to advocate for particular health and safety laws, the definition of rights and responsibilities regarding health and safety is ultimately a political process, subject to competing pressures (e.g., see Epstein 1979; Rabinovitch 1981).

For instance, recombinant DNA technology has created potential economic opportunities for pharmaceutical and bio-

chemical industries. It offers the possibility for new and im-
proved products that will appeal to consumer needs and,
potentially, improve the quality of life. At the same time,
however, the possible hazards of releasing new life forms into
the environment has created a good deal of resistance to the
private development and use of recombinant DNA technology.
Recognition of the public's right to be protected from unknown
hazards presented by new life forms has led to the passage of
laws defining responsibilities relating to the use of recombinant DNA technology and restricting rights to the free use of
and access to new life forms.

The actual definition of rights and responsibilities in relation to any health and safety hazard is a political process in
which competing groups seek to have the law recognize rights
which benefit their own group. Business corporations clearly
have an interest in minimizing the degree to which their use of
technology is restricted. Other groups, which we might call the
potential victims of technological hazards, have an interest in
restricting technology in ways that might harm them. These
groups then compete in the political process to pass laws that
protect their interests. While social scientists agree that the
definition of laws is a political process, they often disagree
about the details of how this political process works. Consequently, social scientists rely on different theoretical frame-
works to explain the creation of laws.

Conflict Theories of Law

Sociologists who subscribe to conflict theories of law argue
that the power elite, made up primarily of leaders within the
corporate sector of American society, wield enough political
power and influence to shape the development of corporate
laws (Domhoff 1979; Mills 1956; Reiman 1990; Chambliss and
Seidman 1982). Conflict theorists argue that the powerful
employ their influence to protect their rights and prerogatives
to engage in business activities and to maximize profits with
minimal restraints. To illustrate their contention that the
corporate sector has a strong influence over law, conflict

theorists point to deficiencies in existing corporate laws, the failure of such laws to protect people from many hazards and the ways in which corporate laws minimize the degree of control and punishment to which members of the power elite are subjected. Other continuing problems, such as occupational exposure to dangerous chemicals, groundwater contamination from inadequate hazardous waste disposal, and the production of unsafe consumer goods, provide evidence for the conflict perspective's claim that the corporate elite use their power to shape laws to their own economic advantage (Simon and Eitzen 1990; Reiman 1990; Box 1983).

Much recent research into how the power elite shapes laws provides further evidence for the position taken by conflict theorists. In recent years, powerful individuals have been very successful in shaping laws, policies and politics through political campaign contributions to Political Action Committees (PACs). Corporations can also use PACs to their advantage, and many corporations donate large sums of money to PACs, which redistribute corporate contributions to individual political leaders and political hopefuls. These politicians owe some allegiance to the corporation or individual that made the original contribution. Evidence suggests that this mechanism has been very effective in influencing the laws politicians support (Simon and Eitzen 1990, 22-26; Mathias 1986; Bolling 1986).

Corporations and industries can also employ well-paid and well-funded lobbyists to influence the law-making process. Corporate lobbyists serve the specific needs of particular industries or companies, and have little concern with national or international interests. The question, as Simon and Eitzen (1990, 22) note, is who speaks for "the relatively powerless" on behalf of society?

By exposing this connection between business and government, we do not mean to imply that a conspiratorial link exists between these two groups. Corporations are not the only group capable of influencing the law, and the law does not always reflect the best interests of the powerful (Chambliss and Seidman 1982). However, given the power of the corporations, they have an advantage over isolated and disorganized individual citizens when it comes to influencing political decision making.

Conflict theory also does not suggest that laws designed to curb corporate violence do not exist. Rather, conflict theorists argue that laws ostensibly designed to protect consumers, workers and the environment that create precautionary duties for business are undermined in other ways. For example, many laws designed to protect the public, consumers or the workforce are rarely enforced (Reiman 1990,102-103; Lynxwiler *et al.* 1983). Other laws, such as anti-trust laws and pure food and drug laws, were actually promoted by businesses to increase public confidence in corporations. Thus, conflict theorists conclude that laws protecting health and safety, which create responsibilities for corporations to protect health and safety, are merely part of "public relations" campaigns. These laws are designed to reassure the public that their health and safety are being protected without really providing any extra measure of safety. For example, a variety of health and safety laws exists. However, the agencies charged with enforcing these laws are so underfunded that they cannot perform their function (Calavita 1983). In essence, business practices remain unchanged by these laws while the public is led to believe that government agencies are protecting the public's interests in health and safety. In short, despite the existence of protection-oriented laws, it is "business as usual" as far as corporations are concerned.

Pluralist Theory of Law

A different point of view is expressed by theorists who adopt a pluralist view of American politics. Rather than viewing law as representing the will and interests of a powerful and stable elite, pluralists view law as the product of a constant tug-of-war between competing groups. In this pluralist competition, the winner is not always the same elite group. Instead, other groups occasionally score victories, gaining new rights and concessions from their opponents in the form of stricter business regulation. Pluralist theorists point to the progress that has been made in corporate crime legislation over the past twenty years as evidence that the corporate elite, while possessing considerable political influence, has not been able to avoid new responsibilities being pressed upon it by mobilized groups of consumers, workers, and environmentalists. Moreover, although many corporate violations go uncorrected and unpunished, these theorists emphasize the increasing number of prosecutions for such offenses.

Pluralist theorists also have offered a variety of explanations, besides corporate sector power, to explain why it has been so difficult to enforce laws aimed at curbing corporate crimes of violence. For example, pluralists note that it is often difficult to detect or obtain sufficient evidence to convict corporations of corporate crimes and that it is this characteristic that makes enforcement less than effective, regardless of how many resources might be devoted to enforcement of these laws.

The Politics of Law

Ultimately, the difference between conflict and pluralist theories is a matter of perspective and degree. Both view law as the product of a power struggle. They simply have different conceptions of the relative power of the parties to the conflict and the magnitude of the victories each side has attained. While some conflict theorists overemphasize the power of the corporate sector (e.g., Quinney 1974), ignoring other important factors influencing political decisions and governmental action, some pluralist theorists have become so caught up in the details of policy implementation and the myriad difficulties that ensue that they lose sight of the constant pressure of corporate sector power under which corporate regulation and policy must be carried out.

These differences aside, it is abundantly clear that corporate law, and therefore what is a corporate crime, is the product of a political process. Through this process, the law defines responsibilities to take precautions against injury and violence.

Because corporate law is the product of a political process, resulting legislation does not always correspond to a rational plan. All sorts of inconsistencies appear in the law. One such inconsistency relates to the types of penalties attached to corporate violence regulated by health and safety laws. While it is convenient to continue referring to the whole class of illegal acts affecting health and safety as "crimes," it is important to recognize that the majority of health and safety laws do not impose *criminal* penalties. Consequently, the violent acts which these laws address are not truly "crimes," but only civil offenses.

Differentiating Crime from Civil Offenses

The principle difference between criminal and civil offenses is in the adjudicatory process, the labelling process and the penalties assigned to defendants. Violators of criminal law receive a highly stigmatizing criminal label which brands the convicted defendant as a criminal and an outcast. Conviction for a civil offense does not carry this extra load of symbolic punishment. In addition, a penalty of incarceration may not be imposed for a civil offense. Finally, because a person cannot be incarcerated for a civil offense, criminal law is commonly perceived as more serious, and as imposing more serious penalties than civil offenses.

At times, these differences between criminal and civil law have generated social, political or legal movements designed to bring corporate violations within the scope of the criminal law. For example, during the 1970s, when many laws regarding health and safety were either strengthened or created, a number of people pushed for the adoption of criminal penalties for violations of health and safety standards. They sought criminal penalties on a number of grounds.

The first argument begins with the observation that perpetrators of health and safety and other forms of corporate violence are often well-to-do executives or corporations. Monetary fines contained within applicable civil laws are easily passed on to consumers as just another cost of doing business (Box 1983, 49; Green 1972). The possibility of going to jail cannot be so easily ignored, however. Therefore, criminal penalties and the possibility of a jail or prison sentence might serve as a greater deterrent than civil penalties (Box 1983, 44-53).

The second argument in favor of criminal penalties rather than civil penalties is that civil penalties cannot deter because they do not contain a sufficient amount of stigma (Vandivier 1982; Geis 1978). As noted above, criminal conviction is believed to carry a social stigma, or a type of social shame. Potential criminals may avoid committing crimes because of the stigma attached to criminal conviction if they get caught. If this is so, the threat of a criminal conviction *and* fine should deter better than a civil fine of the same size because the stigma of criminal conviction is itself something that people will try to avoid.

In relation to corporate crime, however, there is some question about the actual stigmatizing power of criminal sanctions. Box (1983,53) notes, for example, that:

> [t]he majority of executives found guilty of corporate crime not only retain their jobs or have others found for them, but also find that funds to cover their fines are somehow made available. For some,... crime may even pay:... in the Goodrich disc-brake scandal... two of the main executives involved were later promoted.

A third argument in favor of criminal penalties rests on moral grounds. Here, the actions of corporate executives that cause injury and illness are compared to conventional street violence. If muggers and robbers are punished criminally, so should the corporations that cause even greater amounts of harm by ignoring health and safety. A number of criminologists have described workplace illnesses, consumer product accidents, and harmful pollution of the air and water as assault (Reiman 1990; Michalowski 1985; Messerschmidt 1986). Ralph Nader declared that occupational injury and disease were a "domestic form of violence." In this view, criminal penalties are deemed necessary for just retribution on the grounds that civil penalties cannot express the moral outrage and community condemnation merited by these heinous violent acts.

Criminal versus Civil Offenses—Current Law

Because the creation of law is a political process, the advocates of criminal penalties were not always successful in translating their preferences into law. For example, most of the recent laws that attempt to limit corporate crimes of violence include some criminal penalties. However, these penalties frequently were more restricted than the advocates of criminal penalties prefer, and in practice have been used even less. Indeed, the criminal punishments aimed at corporate crimes of violence are often relatively light given the seriousness of the conduct which they address. For example, under the federal Occupational Safety and Health Act (OSHA), intentionally violating health or safety regulations that causes the death of an employee, which is a crime equivalent in severity to manslaughter, may result in a maximum penalty of only six months imprisonment—hardly a serious penalty given the harm that is done.

In almost all instances, criminal penalties for corporate violence are authorized only in the case of a *willful* or *knowing* violation of law. In some cases, the intentional violation must actually result in the *endangerment* or *injury* of someone *before* criminal penalties can be imposed. Considering the nature of corporations, their complex hierarchical structure and secrecy, it is often difficult to muster the type of evidence necessary to prove that the outcome was *intended* and was *knowingly* and *willfully* carried out (e.g., see Cullen *et al.* 1987).

Despite the limited scope of these laws and the difficulty in proving intent, prosecutions for certain corporate crimes of violence have been on the rise. For example, the number of prosecutions for crimes against health and safety for which criminal penalties are possible increased throughout the 1980s, usually against offenders who showed a total disregard for safety and health in the conduct of their business. Some argue that the greater willingness to deal with corporate acts of violence as criminal acts is a reflection of a change in public opinion regarding these acts (Cullen *et al.* 1983, 1984, 1987). Regardless of the reason for this trend, it appears that criminal penalties for corporate violence are increasingly being applied to the most blameworthy offenders. At the same time, however, civil penalties remain the norm.

The Increasing Importance of Civil Penalties

The increased use of criminal penalties has been overshadowed by the tremendous increase in the use of civil penalties. Most laws pertaining to corporate wrong-doings involve the application of regulatory laws by administrative agencies (Meier 1985). For example, the Security and Exchange Commission (SEC) oversees trading of stocks on Wall Street and at other stock exchanges (Shapiro 1984). The Food and Drug Administration (FDA) regulates prescription and over-the-counter drugs, cosmetics, medical devices, and many foods (Meier 1985,82). Other foods, such as meat, poultry and eggs, come under the auspices of the Food Safety and Inspection Service (FSIS; Meier 1985,87). The automobile industry is regulated by the National Highway Traffic Safety Administration (NHTSA; Meier 1985,95). Violations of worker health and safety laws are monitored by the Occupational Health and Safety Administration (see Meier 1985 for list and descriptions of duties of other agencies). These agencies are the "corporate police." However, they often do not have the same authority and resources as the police, and in some instances, cannot charge offenders with criminal violations. These agencies are mainly "administrative" or regulatory.

Typically, the legislature creates administrative regulatory agencies to make specific rules safeguarding health and safety in relation to particular types of hazards. For example, Congress created OSHA to make rules pertaining to worker health and safety and the EPA (Environmental Protection Agency) to create rules protecting the environment. The legislation creating each agency also contains general penalty provisions that spell out the penalties for different types of violations. Generally, the specified penalties provide civil law remedies. However, criminal penalties may also be specified, usually only for the most serious kinds of violations.

In addition to the differences between criminal and civil sanctions described above, another major difference between civil and criminal law concerns the standard of proof necessary for a conviction. Civil law provisions often impose *strict liability*, while criminal penalties are reserved for *intentional* or knowing violations of the law.

Strict liability means that the fault or *intent* of the violator *is not relevant* to establish liability. Consequently, simply violating the law, even by accident or mistake, can still be penalized under civil law. Take, for instance, the laws relating to water pollution. In such cases, civil penalties may be imposed upon anyone dumping illegal hazardous wastes even *if* the person was *unaware* that what was being dumped was hazardous or illegal, and even though the dumping was inadvertent — for example, because an employee opened the wrong valve.

Strict liability is used to make *enforcement easier* and to raise the level of care exercised by persons engaged in potentially hazardous occupations. Proving intent is extremely difficult not only in cases of health and safety violations, but in most cases involving corporate violence. By relying on the principle of strict liability rather than upon criminal law in health and safety cases, the government has a better chance of winning such cases and penalizing those who create hazards. But strict liability has another role as well: because potential violators are aware that pleading error or accident is not a sufficient legal excuse under these laws, strict liability should motivate potential violators to use extra care to avoid mistakes and accidents which might lead to violations. In short, strict liability is intended to deter such violations.

There are other advantages to civil penalties which tend to make them more attractive than criminal sanctions in cases involving corporate violence. In particular, civil violators are not entitled to the same procedural rights that must be afforded criminal defendants. Thus, civil offenses are more easily prosecuted.

It should be clear at this point that corporate violence is subject to a *dual system of justice* that involves civil as well as criminal penalties. The fact that two types of sanctions can be applied to corporations requires that those who enforce administrative regulations make a choice. Thus, there is a great deal of discretion involved in charging corporate defendants under current administrative laws.

Discretionary Enforcement

Strict liability allows administrative agencies to impose civil penalties in almost any instance in which a violation is discovered by government officials (Lynxwiler *et al.* 1983). As a practical matter, however, government officials usually do not pursue these penalties unless the violator appears to have been particularly neglectful or stubbornly refuses to correct a violation which they have brought to the violator's attention. This use of *discretionary enforcement* means that even civil penalties are used primarily in instances of willful violations, when a criminal penalty also might be viewed as appropriate.

The manner in which government officials choose to employ their discretion affects how corporate violations are labelled: whether they are recorded as civil or criminal violations or even ignored entirely. One consequence of this dual set of penalties and the way in which they are applied to violators is that it is difficult, if not impossible, to distinguish between "crimes" committed by corporations and corporations' "civil" violations. Frequently, behaviors that are treated as civil violations could be handled as criminal violations (Sutherland 1949), but are not because of the relative difficulty of obtaining a criminal conviction. This is one reason why our definition of corporate violence includes acts even if they are not violations of the criminal law.

Who is Responsible?

Whether or not the law requires proof of specific intent, the concept of corporate violence requires some degree of blameworthiness on the part of those being penalized. Blame can be assessed on a sliding scale. Somewhere along that scale we may view the behavior as so blameworthy that it deserves criminal sanctions.

One level of blame is the failure to reasonably investigate the potentially harmful consequences of one's actions. How thorough must this investigation be to avoid imputation of blame? For example, how carefully must a manufacturer investigate the possible harmful effects of a product before putting it up for sale? At one time, manufacturers had almost no responsibility to investigate possible hazards. During the twentieth century, societal standards of responsibility have evolved, requiring manufacturers to investigate at least the immediate and direct hazards related to their actions. For instance, manufacturers of drugs, food additives and pesticides have been required to conduct safety tests. Currently, our understanding of hazards is leading some analysts to conclude that producers have a responsibility to investigate and take into account the long-term and indirect consequences of their production decisions. Many of the worst ecological and health hazards stem from what happens to a product after it has been consumed. Plastic six-pack holders choke and kill aquatic mammals when discarded improperly or even when disposed of in landfills. Paint thinners and other chemicals contaminate ground water when they are dumped down household drains and industrial sewers.

In time, new concepts of responsibility may evolve, requiring an investigation of the full range of potentially dangerous impacts of corporate decisions. For example, corporations may be required to investigate the potential hazards of their products "from cradle to grave," including the hazards associated with the production of the raw materials for the product and with disposal of the product. This is the goal of the ecological or green movement, for example.

The next level of blame is when a person or corporation is responsible for a harm, knows about it, and does little to prevent the harm. How little is too little? Are there reasonable alternatives? At what point do the costs of preventing the harm exceed the seriousness of the harm itself, thereby justifying the continuation of the hazardous activity? These issues are raised by many of the examples explored in this book.

It is not always possible to place blame. Some harms are unavoidable. Even the most careful investigations of possible harms may overlook something. We need to guard against the impulse to point a finger of blame for every harm that we discover. Some serious harms may be no one's fault. The fact that a harm exists does not necessarily mean that some individual or corporation is blameworthy. Even if the actions of the corporation cause the harm, the corporation may not be morally blameworthy and may not deserve criminal punishment. Furthermore, even in cases in which blame can be assessed, criminal sanctions may not offer the most effective remedy.

Anatomy of a Corporate Crime

Consider, for example, the responsibility for worker safety violations. A common cause of worker injuries is work speed-ups that require workers to complete tasks very quickly. The scenario leading to an "accident" may go something like this. Top corporate management needs to fill orders within a certain deadline. Several options are available. They could hire extra workers to increase the rate of production, they could pay their regular workers to work overtime to increase production, or they could indicate to plant management that it will be necessary to make workers produce more during regular working hours. At no point do corporate managers consider lowering worker safety practices or trading a few injuries for the necessary increase in productivity. They simply inform plant managers of the need to increase production to meet outstanding orders.

The plant manager passes along this information to supervisors who in turn tell employees that they will need to meet particular production goals. The assembly line is speeded up. With the speed-up, workers experience greater fatigue, sore muscles and stiff joints and an increasing number of back injuries. As they become more and more worn out, workers may look for ways to make their work easier. Some may dismantle safety guards and other safety devices which, though designed to protect the worker, also make the work more cumbersome. The supervisor notices that the safety mechanism has been dismantled, and reminds the worker that it should be replaced. Knowing that the entire assembly line would have to be shut down temporarily while the device is put back in place, the supervisor tells the worker to replace the safety device at the end of the day. A few hours later, the worker's hand gets caught in the machine.

Who is responsible? Is it the worker who took the safety device off the machine? Is it the supervisor for failing to require that the device be replaced immediately? Is it the plant manager for failing to inform corporate management that increasing production, without extra personnel or extra hours, would be unsafe? Is it corporate management for failing to maintain an organization in which safety is the primary concern and production goals always come second? Is it the corporate stockholders who are responsible for failing to communicate the importance of safety to corporate officers? Is it the corporation for pursuing profit beyond human capabilities?

The recent Alaskan oil spill caused by the Exxon *Valdez* illustrates these issues exceptionally well. On March 24, 1989, an Exxon oil tanker ran aground in Prince William Sound off of the coast of Alaska, creating an environmental disaster of enormous proportions. Eleven million gallons of crude oil contaminated the water and beaches, destroying marine habitat and contaminating fish that otherwise would be used as food. Alaskan prosecutors issued criminal charges against the captain of the vessel within days after the spill. Captain Joseph Hazelwood faced a possible prison sentence of twelve years if convicted on all charges.

One question remains, however: was Captain Hazelwood solely responsible for the grounding of the Exxon *Valdez*? A *Time* magazine investigation (and later on the courts) concluded that Hazelwood was not the only one to blame for the accident. They questioned Exxon's failure to recognize that Captain Hazelwood had a drinking problem and Exxon's sharp cuts in the size of tanker crews that resulted in crew members working fatiguing shifts of twelve to fourteen hours. In addition, the failure of the Coast Guard to spot the ship before it got into trouble is also implicated in the cause of the grounding (*Time* 1989). Further, the Valdez was a single-hulled ship. This meant that damage to the outside hull would result in an oil spill. Many oil companies now use double-hull ships to prevent oil spills. Exxon chose not to spend the additional money necessary to protect the environment by purchasing double-hulled ships for its oil transportation fleet.

Some legal experts have argued that criminal penalties should be imposed against the Exxon corporation. One former prosecutor believed that "prosecutors should treat this as a violent crime against the community." He pointed to the fact that the captain had previously had his automobile driving license suspended for drunk driving. Exxon, he argued, had not taken appropriate care in identifying the captain as a potential hazard because of his history of drunk driving. Another former prosecutor took the argument one step further, noting that the federal government should also bear some of the blame because it did not have sufficient clean-up equipment available in good working condition. "With that many ships coming through the area," he said, "the lack of availability of ships reeks of negligence" (Berg 1989, 1).

Questions like these could be asked with respect to most corporate crimes of violence. Another way to ask the question is: *Who should be penalized?*

Oftentimes, societal concepts of responsibility lead us to view corporate violence as "accidents" and hold no one responsible (Lynch *et al.* 1989). Blame is not distributed. No one is punished, and questionable practices continue to flourish unfettered. A different approach is to acknowledge that responsibility is diffused within corporations and to hold the *corporation* as a whole legally responsible. Like the evolving standards of blame, concepts of corporate responsibility have evolved over time.

Punishing Corporations

Corporate criminal responsibility has been an issue of increasing academic interest in recent years (Coffee 1981). In addition, several court decisions have broadened the potential for corporations to be held criminally responsible for the violations that occur within them. While corporate criminal responsibility has helped to resolve some of the difficult questions of who is to blame, it has raised a number of difficult problems of its own.

One of the principle objections to corporate criminal responsibility is that the wrong people get punished. The pain of corporate criminal punishments can easily be passed on to others. Consequently, consumers, stock holders and employees are the ones who get punished. Consumers end up paying higher prices for the products made by the corporation. The corporation's stockholders, who had no knowledge of the decisions that led to the injury, may see their dividends fall or the value of their stock decrease.

The corporation's employees may experience lay-offs and reduced wages. Thus, others argue that punishing entire corporations is not the answer.

Punishing Key Personnel

An alternative to corporate criminal responsibility is to hold particular "key" individuals responsible for whatever violations occur within the corporation (Stone 1975, 58-69). In some corporations, particular positions, such as sanitation supervisor, safety engineer, or compliance officer, are designed to channel legal liability in the event of a violation. These arrangements have led some commentators to refer to these positions as "vice presidents in charge of going to jail." Often these key employees do not possess the corporate authority to stop the violations. As a result, they become "whipping-boys," shielding the responsible corporate officials from punishment.

Fair and Effective Penalties

Society's notions about fair and effective remedies are shaped by social, economic, and political forces. For example, the same forces that create mountains of trash in our "throwaway society" also shape our views about the reasonableness of our consumption patterns and the feasibility of alternatives. The annual death toll on our nation's highways may seem justified by the freedom it offers us. But it may seem reasonable only in the absence of convenient and affordable mass transit systems. Economic and political forces, in turn, perpetuate our society's unwillingness to invest in mass transit. Powerful economic forces, particularly represented by the automotive and petroleum industries, have encouraged the investment in highways rather than railroads. Focusing on the micro-level issue of blame for automobile deaths may prevent an understanding of the macro-level issues of investment in mass transit.

In some situations, however, blame is entirely appropriate and punishment may lead to a decrease in similar acts by other corporations. It is up to the discretion of enforcement officials to choose the type of intervention that will both reflect community values and offer effective deterrents to future violations. Whether this discretion is used wisely is, of course, another matter.

Four

Conventional Laws for Unconventional Crimes

CORPORATE CRIMES DIFFER from traditional street crimes in many respects. As previously noted, one difference relates to the manner in which corporate and street criminals come into contact with the legal system. Street criminals enter the criminal justice system because they have violated a criminal law and are apprehended by the police. Corporate criminals, however, come into contact with the legal system through several mechanisms, including civil, administrative and criminal law violations. The majority of corporate violations are pursued civilly and administratively. Few corporate crimes are pursued criminally. Thus, it is instructive to examine how the criminal law is applied to corporations and corporate executives who commit violent crime.

Not all corporate crimes of violence are treated as equally serious. Many criminal prosecutions are initiated when corporations violate regulatory laws, usually because of repeated and willful violations. The most dramatic and rare corporate crime prosecutions involve corporate executives charged with homicide for their neglect of safety precautions. These prosecutions raise several issues and require that we take a hard look at our values. One issue that needs to be addressed is deciding what we mean by criminal homicide and the kinds of conduct that deserve to be punished as criminal homicide.

To address this issue, this chapter presents several cases where corporations or corporate executives were charged with criminal homicide. The first involves the prosecution of Ford Motor Company for reckless homicide in the celebrated Pinto case. This case includes elements of high drama: the small-town prosecutor with few resources, supported by volunteer workers and law students taking on an industrial giant almost single-handedly. It also presents some important legal and moral questions relative to the punishment and control of corporate crimes of violence.

The second case examines the conviction of three executives on charges of murder in the death of an employee from cyanide fumes in a plant operated by these executives. This is the first case in which corporate officials were charged with murder for the job-related death of an employee.

Since these ground-breaking cases, a number of other cases have been brought charging corporations or corporate executives with homicide. We review some of these cases and the current status of homicide prosecutions against the corporate sector.

THE EXPLODING FORD PINTO

> On August 10, 1978, Judy and Lyn Ulrich and their cousin..., Donna Ulrich, set out to play volleyball at a church some twenty miles away. While on U.S. Highway 33 in northern Indiana, the yellow 1973 Pinto they were driving was struck from the rear by a van. Within seconds their car was engulfed in flames. Two of the teenagers, trapped inside the vehicle, died quickly; the driver, Judy, was thrown clear of the blazing Pinto with third-degree burns on more than 95 percent of her body. Though conscious following the accident, she died at a hospital eight hours later (Cullen, *et al.* 1984, 111).

Under normal circumstances, the explosion of the Ulrichs' Pinto might have been regarded as a freak accident. Information surrounding this incident, however, suggested that this was no accident, in the sense that an accident is a more or less random and unpredictable event. This tragic crash was only one in a series of fiery crashes across the country involving Ford Pintos. Investigations by Mark Dowie of *Mother Jones* magazine and subsequent tests by the National Highway Traffic Safety Administration (NHTSA) revealed that Ford Pintos contained a design defect which caused them to explode when hit from the rear, even at relatively low speeds. A NHTSA investigation uncovered 38 cases in which rear-end Pinto collisions resulted in fuel leakage and fire, and caused 27 deaths and 24 burn injuries (Strobel 1980, 20). In NHTSA crash tests, two Pintos "exploded into flames" when hit from behind at 35 miles per hour (Cullen *et al.* 1987, 165). Dowie (1977, 18) estimated that "Pinto crashes have caused 500 burn deaths to people who would not have been seriously injured if the car had not burst into flames." In one such incident, Richard Grimshaw, 13, "suffered burns over 90 percent of his body and lost his nose, his left ear, and much of his left hand" (Cullen *et al.* 1987,163).

Design defects which could cause injury and death are not uncommon, but we expect manufacturers to prevent and, when discovered, to correct such defects. Ford did not act to correct known defects in Pintos. Dowie and others had collected information and internal Ford documents which strongly suggested that Ford Motor Company executives knew about the design defect from the early stages of Pinto production and decided that the cost of correcting the defect, estimated to be from $5 to $11 per car, was too high:

> Ford executives made the decision not to guard against potential fuel-leakage problems caused by the placement of the Pinto's gas tank, which made it vulnerable to puncture in rear-end collisions. In an internal company memo dated April 22 [1971], it was recommended that Ford defer adoption of the flak suit or bladder on all affected cars until 1976 to realize a design cost savings of $20.9 million compared to incorporation in 1974 (Cullen *et al.* 1987, 159-160).

Armed with these documents, which had been instrumental in a recent $128 million civil judgment against Ford (Strobel 1980, 21), the Elkhart County prosecutor convened a grand jury. After hearing testimony from Ford officials and safety experts, the grand jury unanimously agreed to charge Ford Motor Company with reckless homicide (Cullen *et al.* 1984, 116). The grand jury held that the Pinto design defect which prompted the Elkhart County prosecutor to bring three counts of reckless homicide against the Ford Motor Company was willful. A tragic mistake might be forgiven. Willful recklessness could not.

At trial, the central issues were: (1) whether Ford Motor Company, having prior knowledge of the design defect in Pintos, had a responsibility to repair or warn Pinto owners of this hazard, and (2) whether Ford recklessly disregarded this duty (Maakestad 1983, 859-860).

Although conviction on these three charges could result in a maximum fine of only $30,000, Ford had ample reason to be concerned about the charges and to defend itself vigorously. The potential financial impact of conviction far exceeded the fines that the court could impose. The indictments brought front-page headlines and bad publicity. Moreover, a criminal conviction would provide strong evidence for other victims of Pinto crashes suing Ford for damages (Cullen *et al.* 1987, 179-180). Realizing this, Ford spared no expense or effort in preparing its criminal defense.

Ford's defense strategy amply illustrates the advantages accruing to criminal defendants for whom, relatively speaking, money is no object. Ford spent over $1 million dollars in its defense (Strobel 1980, 144), conducting additional crash tests of Pintos and other vehicles ($80,000), and purchasing daily transcripts of the trial ($50,000; see Cullen *et al.* 1984). In the end, it was money well spent for Ford.

The Prosecution's Evidence

The prosecution's case rested on Ford memos and documents regarding crash tests of the Pinto conducted on 1971 and 1972 models and Ford's non-response to low-impact rear-end collision tests on Pintos. While crash test results showed that

Pintos (and their equivalent, Mercury Bobcats) had a tendency to explode when hit from the rear even at low speeds, additional crash tests showed that minor and inexpensive design modifications would greatly reduce the likelihood of a ruptured gas tank in rear-end collisions. Internal Ford documents showed that Ford knew this but chose not to make these modifications because they were considered too costly.

Ford challenged the admission of crash tests and internal memos in court on the grounds that the tests which the prosecution intended to admit into evidence did not pertain directly to the 1973 model Pinto involved in the Ulrich case. The judge agreed with the defense and excluded nearly all materials relating to previous years' models. As a result, only a small fraction of the documentary evidence which the prosecution had collected was admitted into evidence at trial.

Consequently, the prosecution was forced to rely on two remaining lines of evidence. First, the testimony of "auto safety experts, including a former Ford executive who testified that the fuel tank on the Pinto was placed in a potentially lethal position" (Cullen *et al.* 1984, 124). Second, eyewitness testimony establishing that the rear-end impact occurred at a relatively low speed. This testimony would support the prosecutor's claim that the accident would have been a relatively minor fender-bender if not for the defect in the Pinto (Cullen *et al.* 1984, 124).

Ford's Defense

Ford presented its own auto safety experts who testified that 1973 Pintos met prevailing federal automotive safety standards and were just as safe as comparable subcompacts built at that time (Cullen *et al.* 1984, 124). Ford also produced two surprise witnesses who claimed that prior to Judy Ulrich's death in the hospital, she said her car was stopped on the highway. If this was the case:

> ...the speed at impact would have been 50 miles per hour, a
> collision that no small car could have withstood. This
> reasoning was given added credence when Ford presented
> newly conducted crash tests which showed that at 50 miles

per hour a van would sustain only minimal damage despite the large crushing effect it exerted on the rear of the Pinto (Cullen *et al.* 1984, 124).

Ultimately, the trial's outcome hinged on a legal technicality. A new provision of Indiana's reckless homicide statute, which Ford was being tried under, had gone into effect only forty-one days prior to the crash that killed the Ulrichs. The judge ruled that any reckless conduct prior to the effective date of the statute was not to be considered by the jury. "The elements of the indictment concerning the car's defective and dangerous design were relevant only to establish the reason why Ford should have warned the public or fixed the car during that 41-day period" (Strobel 1980, 58). Thus, because Indiana's law was so new, Ford's reckless conduct in initially manufacturing and selling a car known to contain a dangerous design defect was held to be irrelevant.

Moreover, the Ford Motor Company had announced a recall of Pintos on June 9, 1978, *two months before* the Ulrich's fatal crash. Ford's defense focused on the recall, and presented evidence that Ford moved as quickly as possible to recall Pintos once the new law was in effect.

Outcome and Aftermath of the Pinto Case

After four days of deliberation, the jury found Ford Motor Company not guilty on all charges. In many ways, the trial's result is more a reflection on the peculiarities of the case than the guilt or innocence of the Ford Motor Company. The 41 day limit attached to Indiana's reckless homicide statute prevented the prosecution from trying Ford on recklessness in designing and selling Pintos. Instead, the issue was shifted to whether Ford had behaved recklessly in its recall of Pintos during the 41 days immediately preceding the accident.

Legally, the impact of the case has been much less spectacular than predicted by legal pundits. The case has not opened a floodgate of corporate criminal prosecutions, and instead stands as a grave lesson to prosecutors who might consider bringing criminal charges against a large corporation. The Elkhart County prosecutor's office total annual budget of $200,000 was already committed to routine office tasks (Strobel 1980, 37). The prosecution obtained a supplementary budget of only $20,000 and the voluntary legal assistance of some interested law professors to try Ford. Ford spent over a million dollars on its defense. As noted earlier, conflict theorists argue that the enormous resources of the corporate sector allow it to shape and manipulate law to protect corporate members from punishment for their immoral and illegal acts. They point to the Pinto case as an example of corporate sector immunity from punishment.

Pluralists, however, argue that the legal impact of this case is less important than its social meaning. The case stands as a landmark in the social definition of crime. When the grand jury in Elkhart charged Ford Motor Company with reckless homicide, it made a moral decision. The behavior of Ford officials in allegedly failing to make necessary changes in Pinto gas tanks despite evidence that Pintos were likely to explode and that repairs would cost less than $15 per car, was deemed the sort of behavior that merited criminal punishment. The prosecution of this case acted as a marker of moral indignation, and indicated that the community will not tolerate such behavior.

A similar moral statement is found in the conviction of three Chicago area executives for their failure to provide appropriate safeguards for their employees.

MURDER IN THE WORKPLACE

Stefan Golab, a Polish immigrant, worked for Film Recovery Systems, Inc., a firm involved in recycling silver from used photographic plates. The recycling process used by Film Recovery involved soaking used X-ray plates in a cyanide solution. Cyanide is highly poisonous if swallowed, inhaled, or absorbed through the skin, and workers must be protected with rubber gloves, boots, aprons, respirators, and effective ventilation. This recycling process is conducted safely by several firms across the country. At the Film Recovery plant, however, normal precautions were not taken. Workers testified that they were given only paper face masks and cloth gloves. Ventilation was so poor inside the plant that the air was thick with the odor of cyanide and a "yellowish haze" of cyanide fumes hung inside the plant (Nelson 1985, 1). Workers frequently became ill, going outside the plant to vomit, returning to their work over fuming cyanide vats. In fact, without proper safety equipment, Golab and other workers in the Film Recovery plant

> chipped the film, mixed the cyanide granules with water in the vats, stirred the chips in the potent mixture for three days with long rakes, scooped the spent—and cyanide soaked—film chips out of the vat with a giant vacuum cleaner, cleaned the tank in preparation for the next load, and scraped the silver from the terminal plates on which it had been recovered (Owens 1985, 31).

On February 10, 1985, Golab staggered from the cyanide tank where he was working, stumbled to the adjacent lunchroom, and collapsed. His fellow workers dragged him outside and called an ambulance while Golab went into convulsions, frothed at the mouth, and passed out (Magnuson and Leviton 1987, 914). When the ambulance arrived at the hospital, Golab was dead.

An autopsy was performed to determine the cause of death. The medical examiner's first incision released a strong almond-like smell from Golab's body, an indication of cyanide poisoning. Subsequent blood tests revealed that Golab's cyanide blood level was 3.45 micrograms per milliliter—a lethal dose.

Investigation

The autopsy findings led to an eight-month investigation, the indictment of five Film Recovery executives on charges of murder and the indictment of Film Recovery Systems, Inc., and two related corporations on charges of manslaughter. Under Illinois law, "A person who kills an individual without lawful justification commits murder if, in performing the acts which cause the death...[s/h]e knows that such acts create a strong probability of death or great bodily harm to that individual or another...." The indictment became the *first* recorded case of an *employer* being charged with *murder* for the *work-related death of an employee.*

The investigation of Film Recovery Systems and subsequent court testimony revealed a grim scenario. A Cook County

Hospital study of Golab's fellow workers, undertaken following his death, found that "at least two-thirds of Film Recovery's workers suffered ten times a month or more from each of four major symptoms of cyanide intoxication—dizziness, the taste of bitter almonds in the mouth, headaches and nausea and vomiting" (Owens 1985). Workers who complained to the foreman and plant manager about feeling ill, were told to "go outside so you can have some fresh air."

Many workers were not aware that they were working with cyanide. According to a former bookkeeper for Film Recovery, illegal aliens who could not read English were chosen to work in the plant: they could not read the warning labels on the drums of cyanide. Several employees observed skull-and-crossbones markings being painted over or burned off the drums. Because company managers had never informed workers of the hazards of working with the chemical, workers who did see the skull-and-crossbones assumed the chemical was dangerous only if swallowed; they did not realize it could be lethal if inhaled or absorbed through the skin.

Defense Arguments

At trial, the defense presented three lines of argument. First, they claimed that plant conditions were safe. Second, that if the plant was unsafe, the defendants were unaware of any hazards. Third, the defense argued that Golab died of causes unrelated to plant conditions, challenged the medical examiner's findings and suggested that perhaps Golab had eaten apple cores, and that the cyanide in his blood came from the apple seeds. To corroborate the defendants' assertions concerning their lack of knowledge of unsafe conditions at the plant, defense counsel indicated that on several occasions the defendants arranged to have family members work in the plant. The defense also noted that the plant had been given a "clean bill of health" by local and federal inspectors prior to Golab's death.

The failure of regulatory agencies to discover the frightful conditions inside the Film Recovery plant is an unfortunate but interesting sidelight to this story. A federal OSHA inspector visited the offices of Film Recovery, Inc., only two and one-half months before Golab collapsed from cyanide poisoning. The inspector never conducted an inspection of the plant, however, because Reagan administration guidelines prohibited inspectors from conducting on-site inspections unless an examination of company safety records revealed a poor accident record. No such records existed: Film Recovery employees were frequently sent home when they became too dizzy and nauseated to work, and the company kept no record of these incidents (Magnuson and Leviton 1987, 930; Owen 1985). In a subsequent inspection following Golab's death, OSHA found 17 safety violations and ultimately fined Film Recovery over $2,000. The company never paid the fine (Magnuson and Leviton 1987, 930).

Aftermath of the Trial

At the close of the trial, Judge Ronald J.D. Banks convicted three executives of murder and fourteen counts of reckless conduct, and convicted two corporations of involuntary manslaughter and fourteen counts of reckless conduct. In supporting his decision, Judge Banks found that plant conditions were entirely unsafe (safety equipment was lacking and workers were not issued safety instructions nor warned about the hazards of working with cyanide). The judge also found that the three convicted defendants were "totally knowledgeable" of the hazards of cyanide and that their failure to provide proper protective equipment created a strong probability of death or great bodily harm:

> Steven O'Neil [defendant and president of Film Recovery] testified…, and I quote, "I was aware of all of the hazardous nature of cyanide." He knew hydrogen cyanide gas was present. He knew hydrogen cyanide gas, if inhaled, could be fatal.

> Charles Kirschbaum [defendant and plant manager] saw workers vomiting. He was given a Material Safety Data Sheet. He read the label, and he knew what it said. He said that he did not wear the same equipment the workers did because he did not do the same work as the workers, even though he testified to the contrary.

> Daniel Rodriguez [defendant and plant foreman] knew the workers got sick at the plant. He testified to that. He could read the label, and he read it many times.

Each defendant was sentenced to twenty-five years in prison and each corporation was fined $10,000. (One of the five originally indicted executives successfully fought extradition from Utah. A second had the charges against him dismissed halfway through the trial. The convicted defendants filed a successful appeal, and the case was remanded for retrial).

The central issue presented by this case is whether, as a matter of policy, it is desirable to equate the behaviors of Film Recovery executives with murder and to punish it as such. Commentators have referred to the charge of murder in this case as "unprecedented", "scary", and "wild". Others, such as Ralph Nader and Christopher Stone, hailed the verdict as an appropriate application of criminal law. Nader applauded the verdict, saying, "There was a courageous prosecutor and a prudent judge who applied the law to the facts, irrespective of the fact that the defendants had three-piece suits" (Gibson 1985, 2). Stone, an expert on corporate responsibility and corporate crime, commented, "I think this case will properly embolden prosecutors to bring corporate criminal cases, and other judges to stop looking the other way" (Gibson 1985, 1).

Others were more skeptical about the desirability of a murder conviction and expressed concern about how this verdict would change traditional legal conceptions of murder. Richard Epstein, a University of Chicago Law School professor, noted, "One has had to show more than just knowledge of a risk of death, but also a hope or intent that the death would come to pass. Knowledge of risk has not been generally sufficient." He continued, "There is the potential here, given the way most industrial accidents take place, that you'd have a credible shot of pursuing a murder case. It would present a very radical change, in nuance and practice, in the criminal law" (Gibson 1985, 2).

Jay Magnuson, a prosecutor who worked on this case, disagreed with Epstein's statement that most industrial accidents could result in a murder case after the Film Recovery

Systems conviction. Magnuson argued that the difference between the Film Recovery case and other industrial accidents is
that Film Recovery Systems' executives failed to exercise "due
diligence" (Magnuson and Leviton 1987, 935). There is an
important distinction between harms that occur despite vigorous prevention efforts and harms that occur when due diligence is not exercised. This failure to exercise "due diligence"
may even rise to the level of murder if the employer, for
example, not only exposes a person to risk of harm, but also
does not care whether or not the person is injured or killed. This
latter depiction is closest to that made by Judge Banks when he
convicted the defendants of murder—murder by indifference
(see Frank 1988).

More Prosecutions in the Future?

Christopher Stone appears to have been correct when he
predicted that successful prosecution of Film Recovery Systems
for murder would "embolden prosecutors." In recent years
prosecutors across the country have investigated possible
homicide charges or have charged corporations and corporate
executives under conventional violent crime statutes for workplace injuries and deaths. These efforts have led to mixed
results.

In November 1987, charges of assault and endangerment
were brought against two owners of a Brooklyn, New York,
thermometer factory where plant workers were allegedly subjected to mercury vapors which had injured one worker and
were endangering other workers in the plant. At trial, the jury
voted to convict the defendants, but the presiding judge set
aside the verdict, ruling that federal occupational safety and
health law "pre-empted" state law, even in a prosecution for
assault or endangerment. The case is being appealed (*Corporate
Crime Reporter* 1988d, 3).

An Illinois appellate court dismissed an aggravated battery
indictment against the Chicago Magnet Wire Corporation,
charged with subjecting workers to toxic chemicals, on similar
grounds. The appellate court ruled that OSHA is the only agency
empowered to charge a company in relation to worker safety

violations (*Corporate Crime Reporter* 1988d, 3). These judicial rulings have cut off the potential for criminal prosecution of corporations and corporate executives who unjustifiably endanger their employees.

Court rulings that federal job safety and health law bar (or pre-empt) state prosecutions under conventional criminal laws may discourage prosecutors from using criminal prosecutions to deter and punish reckless or negligent conduct resulting in the injury or death of employees. Ultimately, the U.S. Supreme Court may have to decide whether Congress intended the OSHA statute to prohibit a state prosecution for murder when the evidence warrants it.

Prosecutors in many states, however, clearly believe that criminal prosecution is appropriate. New York Attorney-General Robert Abrams represented this view in testimony to a House Subcommittee (*Corporate Crime Reporter* 1987a, 3):

> There seems to be some resistance to the idea that an executive who personally handles no weapon more deadly than a ballpoint pen can commit crimes as violent as assault, manslaughter and even murder. I... assure you, however, that injured workers...are fully aware that they have been the victims of violent crimes. People sometimes recover from the most terrible beatings. People never recover from mercury poisoning.

As criminal prosecution of corporations and corporate executives for crimes of homicide, assault, and endangerment become more common, the controversies surrounding these adaptations of the criminal law promise to become more intense, especially when the criminal law is stretched to cover situations never before treated as murder.

Old Laws, New Crimes

In May 1988, a bus carrying 25 teenagers and 2 adults was hit head-on by a pick-up truck and caught fire. All 27 passengers were killed, dying of smoke inhalation. The driver of the pick-up truck, Larry Mahoney, was found to have a blood-alcohol level 2.5 times the legal definition of drunkenness in Kentucky, where the accident took place. Mahoney was promptly charged with 27 counts of murder. Mahoney's recklessness in driving while intoxicated was not, however, to be the only issue of recklessness to arise in this case.

A week after the accident, "Clarence Ditlow,...Director of the Center for Auto Safety, a public interest group..., called on the state of Kentucky to bring homicide charges against the manufacturer of the bus" (*Corporate Crime Reporter* 1988f, 1). Ditlow charged that the bus involved in the accident was one of the last to be produced by the manufacturer before a federal gas tank standard for buses went into effect in 1977. According to Ditlow (*Corporate Crime Reporter* 1988f, 1):

> the prosecuting attorneys ought to bring criminal charges against the bus manufacturer because they knew that the buses made under old standards were inadequate and they could have just as easily delayed the production of that bus a few days and made it meet the standard....Our best judgment in looking at the severity of the crash, is that the gas tank would not have ruptured if it had been a post-1977 bus and thus the kids would not have died...So here was a bus manufacturer that knew a standard was going to take effect on a certain date and was rushing to produce an unsafe bus prior to the date of the standard.

This case raised difficult questions regarding the liability of corporations for murder. Ditlow argued that the bus manufacturer was as reckless as the drunken driver that caused the accident. In effect, the argument is that Mahoney's drunken driving caused the accident, but the bus company's reckless continuation of an unsafe gas tank design caused the deaths of the 27 passengers who died of smoke inhalation when the bus burst into flames because of the ruptured gas tank.

While the risk posed by the gas tank design may have been substantial, a murder charge requires more than risk. The question which must be addressed is whether the risk was one that no reasonable person would take as long as the gas tank was produced under the legal requirements then in effect. Are we to conclude that the risks posed by the gas tank were reasonable up until the day the government promulgated a regulation requiring that after some future date gas tanks must

be made safer? Moreover, what would be the long-term consequences of establishing a legal precedent whereby manufacturers could be held criminally liable for failure to comply with
regulations that have not yet taken effect?

Questions such as these are more than just interesting
discussion questions. If criminal prosecution for risk-taking
becomes more common, prosecutors will have to grapple with
these questions in deciding whether to charge corporations
and their executives with homicide and other crimes of violence. Their answers to these questions are likely to be influenced by the law, the evidence available in a specific case, and
their own subjective judgments about the blameworthiness of
actors involved. Prosecutors must ask themselves: did the
actions and carelessness shown by the potential defendants
merit the stigma of a criminal charge for murder or another
violent crime?

Conclusion

Despite the initial success of Cook County prosecutors in
the Film Recovery case, prosecuting corporate crimes of violence under conventional criminal laws, such as homicide
statutes, remains a rare event with doubtful prospects for
success. What is won at trial may be lost on appeal, as the
prosecutors of Film Recovery Systems discovered. The application of conventional statutes to violent corporate behavior is
still a legal gamble in a very high stakes game. Although it can
be argued that the criminal law serves as an added deterrent
relative to other available civil remedies, it is not clear whether
the extra deterrent effect is proportional to the tremendous
costs of prosecuting such cases.

The more important effect is moral and symbolic. Moral
outrage against wanton recklessness "creates in society a need
to redress the situation, to seek retribution, to deter" through
the application of criminal sanctions (Magnuson and Leviton
1987, 935). These symbolic values are not as clearly communi-
cated through modern, specialized regulations and administrative sanctions that deal with corporate violence in technical
terms. Though criminal penalties may attach to many of these

specialized crimes, the stigma associated with those charges is not the same as the stigma that attaches to a conviction for manslaughter, murder, or reckless homicide. Violations of these specialized laws are examined in the next chapter.

Five

Regulating Health and Safety

IN THE PREVIOUS chapter, we examined rare but dramatic criminal prosecutions involving corporate crimes of violence. This chapter examines a more typical response to corporate crimes of violence that involve the civil and administrative application of health and safety regulations. The majority of violations and prosecutions within this category involve the risk of injury or illness rather than actual injuries or deaths. Regulatory laws deal primarily in probabilities, and are designed to respond to the likelihood that an unsafe condition or product will cause harm (Hohenemser *et al.* 1980). Health and safety regulations cover a broad field, from building codes to the regulation of nuclear facilities (see Table 5.1 for a summary of the activities of federal regulatory agencies). Local, state, and federal agencies frequently have overlapping jurisdiction in these cases. In addition, health and safety regulation is technically complex, and enforcement of these laws is conducted by specialized agencies which are not a part of the regular criminal justice system. This separation and specialization affects how health and safety laws are enforced and the willingness of enforcement officials to utilize criminal sanctions.

Although the varieties of health and safety regulation are almost endless, this chapter will focus on three general categories of regulation: consumer protection, worker health and safety and environmental regulations.

CONSUMER PROTECTION REGULATION

The public is protected by two types of consumer product regulations: those designed to protect consumers from injury or illness and those designed to protect consumers from misrepresentation and fraud. Because this book is concerned with corporate violence, we focus on the first type of regulation. Numerous consumer products have been regulated (most notably food, drugs, cosmetics and medical devices, pesticides and automobiles) to protect the public from injury.

Food Safety Law

Food was one of the first consumer products to come under health regulations. During the late nineteenth century, technological and economic changes in the food industry provided new opportunities for food to be adulterated with dangerous chemicals or for spoiled food to be disguised as fresh (e.g., with chemicals such as boric acid, formaldehyde and hydrochloric acid, Meier 1985, 78). Artificial food colorings, flavorings and additives used to preserve food were not tested for safety (Kallet and Shlink 1933). Some additives, such as saccharin as a sugar substitute and copper as a preservative in canned peas, came under particularly heavy criticism. Increased public concern over the safety of food additives spurred a pure food movement, spearheaded by the chief chemist for the U.S. Department of Agriculture, Harvey Wiley, who exposed a variety of unsafe practices used to adulterate foods and drugs (Meier 1985, 78). Wiley's initiatives to create federal pure food and drug legislation, though widely supported, failed in Congress (1883), and it was not until 1906 that federal laws regulating foods and drugs

TABLE 5.1
FEDERAL AGENCIES REGULATING HEALTH OR SAFETY

Consumer Product Safety Commission (CPSC)—Establishes mandatory safety standards governing the design, construction, contents, performances and labeling of consumer products.

Environmental Protection Agency (EPA)—Regulates air, water, and noise pollution, waste disposal and specific chemicals considered hazardous to people and the environment; registers and regulates pesticides; administers clean-up of hazardous dumps; monitors other potential pollutants.

Nuclear Regulatory Commission (NRC)—Licenses the construction and operation of nuclear reactors and other facilities; licenses the possession, use, transportation, handling and disposal of nuclear materials; develops and implements rules and regulations governing licensed nuclear activities; licenses the export and import of uranium and plutonium.

Occupational Safety and Health Administration (OSHA)—Develops and enforces mandatory job safety and health standards; maintains reporting and record-keeping procedures to monitor job-related illnesses and injuries.

Food Safety and Quality Service—Regulates the meat, poultry, and egg industries for safety and purity by inspecting all meat, poultry and eggs shipped in interstate and foreign commerce.

Food and Drug Administration (FDA)—Regulates the purity and labeling of food, drugs, cosmetics, and medical devices to protect the public against potential health hazards from these products.

Mine Safety and Health Administration—Develops and promulgates mandatory safety and health standards, ensures compliance with such standards, and proposes penalties for violating standards.

Federal Aviation Administration (FAA)—Establishes and enforces rules and regulations for safety standards covering all aspects of civil aviation.

Materials Transportation Bureau—Develops and enforces equipment and operating safety regulations for the transportation of all materials by pipeline; designates substances as hazardous materials and regulates their transportation in interstate commerce.

National Highway Traffic Safety Administration (NHTSA)—Develops mandatory minimum safety standards for domestic and foreign vehicles sold in the United States; develops safety and wear standards for tires.

Source: Adapted from "Regulation: Process and Politics." *Congressional Quarterly*, 1982, 137-143.

were passed (Meier 1985, 79). Consequently, if consumers were to be protected in the late 1800s, it was up to individual states to provide the necessary legislation.

Early food and drug laws were less successful than hoped. These laws were often used to punish fraudulent rather than unhealthful adulteration, and even to discriminate against certain kinds of products and minimize competition between new and old producers (such as banning the sale of oleomargarine). However, while these laws were clearly designed to address the problem of unsafe and contaminated food sold to consumers, little really changed until the 1900s.

In 1905, Upton Sinclair published *The Jungle*, an exposé of conditions in the Chicago meat-packing industry. Although Sinclair had intended the book to bring attention to the deplorable working conditions in the packing plants, most readers were more concerned about the wretched sanitation practices described by Sinclair (1951, 61):

> [T]he beef had lain in vats of chemicals, and men with great forks speared it out and dumped it into trucks, to be taken to the cooking room. When they had speared out all they could reach, they emptied the vat on the floor, and then with shovels scraped up the balance and dumped it into the truck. This floor was filthy, yet they set Antanas with his mop slopping the "pickle" into a hole that connected with a sink, where it was caught and used over again forever; and if that were not enough, there was a trap in the pipe, where all the scraps of meat and odds and ends of refuse were caught, and every few days it was the old man's task to clean these out, and shovel their contents into one of the trucks with the rest of the meat!

The public attention generated by Sinclair's book acted as the catalyst needed to pass federal laws regulating food and drug purity and safety, such as the Food and Drug Act of 1906 and the Meat Inspection Act of 1907 (Meier 1985,79, 87). These federal laws prohibited adulteration of food or drugs and provided a mechanism for the Department of Agriculture to prohibit the use of certain ingredients in food.

Pluralist theorists point to the history of the Food and Drug

Act as an example of the impact that pressure groups can have on the creation of laws regulating corporate sector behavior. At the same time, conflict theories have proven useful in explaining the emergence of food and drug laws. They argue that food and drug legislation was passed (1): because corporate interests did not oppose, and in fact supported such laws (Kolko 1963; Meier 1985, 79, fn 1), (2) because these laws in fact benefitted the corporate sector (federal inspection legitimized corporate practice and gave certain corporations an upper-hand over their competitors, Meier 1985, 79) and, (3) that although legislatively mandated, these laws have *never* been vigorously enforced because strict enforcement *is* opposed by the corporate sector (Frank 1984). The examples below will illustrate this latter view.

Nevertheless, the federal legislation noted above provided a promising beginning for consumer safety. With the onset of World War I, however, consumer issues took a back seat, and it was not until the depression that consumer safety issues reemerged (Meier 1985, 79-80). The major act passed during this era, The Food, Drug and Cosmetic Act of 1938, "provided that new drugs could only be marketed with the approval of the Food and Drug Administration" (Meier 1985, 81). Most other efforts of this era were short-lived (Meier 1985, 81). Until recently, the extent of consumer protection has been minimal, and corporations proceeded largely unfettered.

Food and drug legislation has been periodically amended to address public concerns, even when these changes place a burden on the corporate sector. One of the most important amendments of the food provisions of the 1906 Food and Drug Act is the Delaney amendment. Passed by Congress in 1958, this amendment required the FDA to remove from the market any food additive found to cause cancer in laboratory animals or humans. In recent years, the Delaney amendment has generated controversy, especially when saccharin was found to cause cancer in some laboratory studies. Widespread opposition to the banning of saccharin led Congress to exempt saccharin from the Delaney amendment. Continued scientific disagreement over the validity of animal studies promises to keep the controversy over the Delaney amendment alive.

Drug Safety Law

Drugs were also covered by the 1906 Food and Drug Act. Even so, effective regulation of drugs lagged behind food regulation, even though the safety of drugs was rightly a matter of concern. Many drugs were sold without prescriptions and contained chemicals that were highly unsafe (Kallet and Schlink 1933). Cure-alls and tonics were particularly popular, but consumers were not told what these medicines contained. Even prescription medicines were often adulterated, diluted, or contained dangerous added ingredients.

While the 1906 act gave the federal government authority to proceed against adulterated drugs, it was not until after the "elixir sulfanilamide" disaster of the 1930s that drug safety was seriously regulated. In 1937, an elixir was sold that used a deadly solvent to keep the drug in liquid form. At least 107 deaths were attributed to the product (Quirk 1980). After this incident and in the wake of public demands for reform, the law was changed to require that all new drugs be submitted to tests that established their safety. The Food and Drug Administration was given authority to approve the safety of new drugs and the power to remove drugs from the market if they later proved to be unsafe.

Some years later (early 1960s), the Kefauver Amendment to the drug provisions of the Food, Drug, and Cosmetic Act further expanded the regulation of drugs, requiring that all drugs must be effective as well as safe before they may be sold. The Kefauver Amendment is also interesting because of the tactics employed to gain support for the bill. The Amendment was opposed by the American Medical Association, which led to a less restrictive bill being introduced (Meier 1985, 83). The less restrictive version of the bill drew wide support from industry and did not require that the safety of new drugs be proven. To counteract this, Kefauver released information to the media concerning the Merrill Corporation's attempt to market thalidomide in the U.S., a drug widely used in Europe and proven to cause serious birth defects. Kefauver showed that under the less restrictive bill, Merrill would have been able to market thalidomide in the U.S.;

the Kefauver Amendment would protect the public from such unsafe drugs. The resulting media coverage of this debate caused President Kennedy to shift his support from the less restrictive bill to Kefauver's proposal (Meier 1985; Nadel 1971; Quirk 1981). The Kefauver Amendment subsequently passed both the House and Senate unanimously.

CRIMINAL PROSECUTION OF FOOD AND DRUG VIOLATIONS

There are two types of crimes related to the safety of food and drugs: (1) production of food, drugs, cosmetics, or medical devices under conditions creating a risk of contamination or malfunction and (2) fraudulent reporting of safety test results.

Criminal Contamination

An extensive regulatory apparatus exists to assure the sanitary production of food, drugs, and cosmetics (Meier 1985, 77-95). The production of food, particularly milk, as well as drugs and cosmetics, must be conducted in accordance with very specific sanitary standards. Dairy plants are inspected twice each year and samples of milk are tested continuously for bacteriological contamination. Under federal law, food processing plants that produce food for interstate sale are inspected annually and must follow strict regulations regarding sanitary conditions. Most states also maintain their own inspection system for food sold within the state.

Given this extensive system of regulation and inspection, food is generally assumed to be safe to eat. However, there are severe shortcomings in this regulatory system which make this assumption unwarranted (see Chapter 8). Moreover, food processors are sometimes tempted to skimp on cleaning or to delay the replacement of equipment. If these violations are not caught by regulatory officials, "accidents" can happen. For example, the nation's attention was briefly directed to the risk of food poisoning in the spring of 1985 when thousands of people became ill and several people died when they drank milk contaminated with salmonella, a bacteria that causes severe flu-like symptoms that, in severe cases, can lead to death. Widespread concerns currently exist over conditions in the poultry industry. More recently, inspectors at the U.S. Department of Agriculture have claimed that the "USDA seal of approval no longer guarantees that chicken is safe to eat..." (*Tallahassee Democrat* 1991, 1a). One inspector claimed that "Chicken we would routinely condemn 10 years ago are now getting through to the consumer...[P]eople are paying taxes for us to do this job and we can't do it. We are not being allowed to protect the consumer" (*Tallahassee Democrat* 1991, 5a). Chickens contaminated with maggots, feces, unseen bacteria and diseases that cause food poisoning (through salmonella and campylabacter) regularly make it to the marketplace (*Tallahassee Democrat* 1991, 5a). Increased public demand for lower fat meats like chicken have led to mass production of chickens in crowded and disease-ridden conditions. Mass slaughter of chickens in mechanized plants easily spreads disease and bacteria from one slaughtered bird to the next. At the same time, less than 0.5 percent of chickens are condemned as unsalable, down from 10 percent in more sanitary conditions ten years ago (*Tallahassee Democrat* 1991, 5a). The industry's own inspection and quality control systems seem to be lacking.

The most recent food "scandal" involves fish. A six month investigation of fresh fish and shellfish by *Consumer Reports* (1992 a, b, c) indicates that the fish we eat is not as safe as we think. This news comes at a time when people are eating more fish than ever before in an attempt to improve their health. *Consumer Reports* (1992a, 103 and 105) notes that "[n]early half the fish...tested was contaminated by bacteria from human or animal feces....[F]ecal [contamination is]...not normally found on finfish....[and] were most likely introduced as the result of poor sanitary practices during processing or distribution...." Forty-four percent of the fish in the sample contained evidence of fecal contamination (*Consumer Reports* 1992a, 105). Twenty-two percent of the samples contain fecal bacteria counts that were a "cause for serious concern" (*Consumer Reports* 1992a, 105). In 40 percent of the fish tested by *Consumer Reports* bacterial analysis indicated that the fish had begun to spoil when purchased. Thirty percent of the fish contained enough bacteria to indicate that the "fish should be headed for the grave instead of the dinner plate" (*Consumer Reports* 1992a, 104). Consumer Reports also found that some fish were contaminated with PCBs and mercury, serious health threats to humans in consistent doses (*Consumer Reports* 1992b, 110-112).

Part of the problem, as *Consumer Reports* notes, is that the "Federal government sets no standards for the number of fecal coliform permissible in raw fish." Consequently, it is up to local understaffed and underfunded agencies to perform the inspections. Further, when a violation is detected, the fines are minimal (*Consumer Reports* 1992b, 113). Fish wholesalers and retailers can, however, obtain a USDA seal of approval by voluntarily participating in an inspection program and paying for the costs of inspection (*Consumer Reports* 1992, 108).

Drugs, cosmetics, and medical devices are also supposed to be produced under conditions that prevent contamination of the product and ensure quality control. Antibiotics that are contaminated with viruses, cosmetics that are contaminated with caustic substances, or medical devices prone to failure could cause serious harm to the users of these products. A recent case (1990) involved the drug desipramine, an anti-depressant, that was contaminated with warafin, a blood thinning agent. People taking contaminated desipramine were likely to suffer severe internal hemorrhages (*Consumer Reports Buying Guide* 1991, 380). Regulations are designed to promote good manufacturing practices and strict quality control in order to prevent these "accidents" from happening.

Case Study

In some cases, violations are not accidental, but purposeful. Corporate officials have been caught violating regulations and knowingly endangering health and safety. An example involves Cordis Corporation, a manufacturer of heart pace-makers.

Pace-makers, medical devices implanted to regulate irregular heartbeats, are regulated by the Food and Drug Administration. For about 1-2 percent of pace-maker wearers, failure of the pace-maker creates a risk of death (Mintz 1989, 33). Nonetheless, Cordis sold thousands of defective pace-makers despite the knowledge of company officials that the devices were prone to failure.

In 1983, an anonymous letter was sent to the Food and Drug Administration concerning "alarming, undisclosed defects in thousands of implanted pace-makers" manufactured by Cordis. An internal Cordis report had uncovered 134 cases of "premature battery depletion" which could result in unexpected power failure (Mintz 1989, 33). Six weeks later (December 2, 1983), Cordis notified the FDA that "it was going to send physicians an 'urgent medical device notification' that the batteries in the Gamma units could die prematurely" (Mintz 1989, 33). The next day the FDA launched an investigation which disclosed that Cordis had done a study of battery failure, but had not evaluated the data or written a report of the findings until Cordis began receiving letters from physicians reporting failures. The FDA study showed that the batteries lasted, on average, only half as long as Cordis claimed.

Additional letters received by the FDA asserted that "Executive management constantly mandates that [an] inferior product be produced without regard for quality or federal laws in order to meet production goals" (quoted in Mintz 1989, 33). A second letter said that the

> new Orthocor...pacer is plagued with problems. Several dogs have died with the unit implanted....Corporate officials want this on the market at all cost. They are aware of the flaws and the very real possibility of patient death and have ignored them. They have altered test data and changed reports to indicate the pacer works... Please stop this device, it is a killer (quoted in Mintz 1989, 33).

A year later, FDA Commissioner Frank E. Young received yet another letter stating, "Sometimes orders come from top management to use some questionable batteries rejected by quality control...they are playing with human life" (quoted in Mintz 1989, 33).

Meanwhile, additional evidence of pace-maker defects, company culpability, and a cover-up were disclosed by the FDA investigation and a Senate investigative hearing. On at least two occasions Cordis officials lied to FDA investigators. On one occasion, Cordis officials falsely claimed that internal reports requested by the FDA had been routinely destroyed. Later, in response to threats of regulatory action, Cordis found a copy of the "destroyed" reports (Mintz 1989, 34). On another occasion, Cordis gave FDA investigators a false copy of a memo from which eight serious potential problems with the pace-makers had been deleted. An FDA investigator testified to the Senate that "an un-named corporate officer told him the purpose of the alteration was to derail the possibility of a full-blown FDA probe by playing down the gravity of Cordis' internal investigation of the battery problem" (Mintz 1989, 34).

The investigation also disclosed that in 1980 Cordis received 10 complaints of "a wiring defect that could induce a short-circuit and cause sudden failure. The defect had the potential to kill a fully dependent wearer" (Mintz 1989, 34). Cordis corrected the defect but did not repair over 2000 units in inventory, which it continued to ship to consumers for almost a year.

In April 1989, Cordis plead guilty to 25 criminal violations, including 13 felonies, "agreed to pay the maximum fine of $623,000, plus $141,000 to reimburse the government for its investigative costs, and to pay the government $5 million for the civil fraud of selling defective pace-makers to the Veterans' Administration and the Department of Health and Human Services" (Mintz 1989, 33). Four former executives were also indicted and scheduled to go to trial in September 1989 on 43 criminal charges.

Despite the ultimate success of the investigation, critics have charged that the FDA "was dragging its feet" in conducting the investigation (Mintz 1989, 33). "Although FDA investigators recommended in February 1985 that the Justice Department take the case before a grand jury, FDA officials did not refer the matter to Justice until November 1986—21 months later" (Mintz 1989, 33). During that period Cordis conducted an internal investigation, fired four executives, and adopted a more cooperative and less confrontational posture toward the FDA (Mintz 1989, 33). Ultimately, Cordis "cooperated with the grand jury investigation" that led to indictments against four executives and the corporation. Cordis also sold its pace-maker division in 1987. This cooperation apparently induced federal prosecutors to recommend a plea agreement with Cordis that would have resulted in total fines of only $123,000 (Mintz 1989, 33). The judge, "in a highly unusual step," rejected this initial plea bargain as "too lenient" (Mintz 1989, 33).

This case demonstrates a number of issues related to regulatory enforcement of health and safety laws and corporate violence. First, although the corporation and corporate executives were charged criminally, the crimes with which they were charged were violations of specialized statutes relating to the regulation of food and drugs and obstruction of a government investigation. Despite the risk of death posed by the defective pace-makers, Cordis was not charged with homicide or endangerment under conventional criminal statutes. If, however, evidence became available that someone did die due to pacemaker failure, a state prosecutor would still have the opportunity to bring conventional criminal charges against the corporation or responsible corporate officials.

Second, critics of the FDA and Justice Department handling of this case point to slow reaction time of government agencies in responding to regulatory violations. Enforcement officials put a great deal of emphasis on the "cooperation" displayed by the corporation after 1985. This cooperation almost seems to have excused the earlier obstruction by the corporation. Chapter 8 will discuss the reasons for this reaction of regulatory officials in greater detail.

The Cordis example illustrates the limitations of corporate self-regulation. Fraudulent safety testing is a specific type of crime against health and safety that can lead to violence.

Safety Testing

Federal food and drug regulations rely on pre-testing of new products for safety and, in the case of drugs, for efficacy. A major category of food and drug violations concerns fraudulent reporting of laboratory and clinical tests conducted to establish the safety of a food additive or drug. The MER/29 scandal reported in Chapter 1 is one example of the ways in which dangerous products may be placed on the market.

In the 1930s, prior to amendments which required the testing of new drugs and food additives, the public was exposed to unknown hazards. The seriousness of the problem was highlighted in an expose entitled *100,000,000 Guinea Pigs*, referring to the nation's population of one hundred million (Kallet and Schlink 1933). Although the law has been changed, ostensibly to protect the consuming public from untested and potentially dangerous food additives and drugs, the law is frequently frustrated.

In 1982, *Mother Jones* magazine investigated the safety testing industry. The investigation concluded that the law offers only the "illusion of safety," and that widespread abuse of testing processes resulted in the government approving products on the basis of inadequate, erroneous, and fraudulent test results. For instance as Dowie (1982) noted:

> At Industrial Bio-Test Laboratories of Illinois, which performed more than 22,000 chemical safety tests in the country, at least 80 percent of some 900 tests examined by the government, conducted on chemicals used in everything from crop pesticides to deodorant soaps, were determined invalid—with evidence that some were deliberately falsified. In the course of investigation, government officials discovered that vital records had been shredded. It will be at least 30 years before IBT's results are evaluated and we can be certain that all the products are safe. Well-respected doctors, prominent in their communities, have repeatedly placed their own patients at risk and endangered the rest of us by bending research protocol and federal rules in the testing of drugs and chemicals on human beings.
>
> A federal task force investigating animal tests of drugs and food additives made by G.D. Searle and Co. found deficiencies in safety tests performed by the company on its own products. In one study, the deaths of particular test animals show up as having occurred more than once in data. In addition, tumors were removed from test animals during the course of the study, an unacceptable practice in the studies of chemical long-term effects.

> For the past five years, millions of dollars of the National
> Cancer Institute's annual budget has been spent on
> research that has since been found to be either fraudulent
> or irrelevant.

Industrial Bio-Test Laboratories, Inc. (IBT), a major testing firm whose clients included 31 of the largest pharmaceutical and pesticide producers in the world, is portrayed as a habitual offender. In 1976, an FDA pathologist discovered that IBT's tests on a drug called Naprosyn were suspicious. Of 160 rats entered in the study, most were not adequately examined for evidence of pathology because the dead rats' bodies were too badly decomposed. In other words, poor handling of laboratory animals destroyed the basis for making any judgment about the safety of the drug. When government investigators began to target IBT for a grand jury investigation, IBT shredded records of hundreds of studies. As a result, "seven long-term studies on the cancer causing potential of cyclamates,...herbicides, and plastics were destroyed" (Dowie 1982, 42). In the continuing investigation, government investigators discovered that in tests on triclocarbon (TCC), a common ingredient of deodorant soaps, new rats were entered into studies to replace animals that had died (Dowie 1982, 42). Four former employees, including the president and chief toxicologist, were convicted on charges of falsification of data and mail fraud. Two defendants received sentences of 6 months in jail and 2 years probation. The president of the company was sentenced to a year and a day in prison and four years probation. IBT, Inc., is now out of business (*New York Times* 1984, p. A22).

A new twist on this same theme occurred during the summer of 1989 when federal investigators disclosed instances of fraud and bribery by pharmaceutical companies seeking certification of generic substitutes for brand-name drugs.

Other Consumer Safety Laws

Food additives and drugs have not been the only consumer products affected by inadequate and fraudulent testing. Pesticides, chemicals used in manufacturing, electrical equipment and appliances, and consumer products such as playground equipment and automobiles, have also been subject to these abuses. These products fall under the jurisdiction of the EPA (Environmental Protection Agency), OSHA, the FTC (Federal Trade Commission), the NHTSA, the CPSC (Consumer Product Safety Commission), and various state regulatory agencies. In some cases, prior testing is required. In other cases, the agency has authority to remove from the market or otherwise regulate those products which have been found to be dangerous. In any case, fraudulent testing subjects consumers to unknown hazards.

To deal with fraudulent testing and the marketing of unsafe consumer products, many agencies request that companies recall products that have been proven to be unsafe in actual use. Product recalls have become a very widespread means of controlling the public's exposure to faulty and dangerous products. Recalled product included everything from cars to drugs and children's toys. Table 5.2 contains a few examples of the many recalls instituted within the U.S. over the past few years.

One problem with recalls as a remedy is that companies generally face no other penalties, even though they may make millions of dollars by selling faulty and dangerous products that cause violence (injury and death, severe burns, etc.). A second problem is that recalls are generally voluntary. Voluntary recalls are widely used, especially by certain agencies like NHTSA (Barnet 1981). For example, Firestone had serious problems with its Firestone 500 steel belted radial tires. The steel belts separated from the tires and led to "thousands of accidents, hundreds of injuries, and 34 known fatalities" (Mokhiber cited in Simon and Eitzen 1990, 121). At one point, Firestone refused to "voluntarily" recall 11 million tires on the market at the request of the federal government. Instead, Firestone stepped up its advertising campaign, and "dumped its remaining 500s onto the market at clearance prices" (Simon and Eitzen 1990, 121). In the end, Firestone was fined a token $50,000.

Referring back to Table 5.2, ask yourself if Pontiac could produce Fieros for 4 years and not know that they were potentially dangerous? Or if Ford could produce approximately

TABLE 5.2

RECENT RECALLS

Model Year/ Company	Reason Recalled	Potential Results	Number Sold
BMW 1988-90	Front Safety Belt Defects	fail in minor crashes causing injury	62,000
1986-on Slinky Pull-Toys	Red lead paint	children could ingest lead causing illness	thousands (unstated)
J.C. Penny Food Processor	food processor may start unexpectedly	amputations	1,400,000
Toastmaster 4 slice toaster	defective switch	electrocution/ burns	8,887
1989-90 Chrysler Dodge Plymouth	cars, trucks and vans with 4 cylinders subject to fires	severe burns/ death	625,000
1985-87 Ford Escort	Front seat not secured properly	cause accidents or severe injury in an accident	1,367,500
1991 Ford Escort	Throttle may stick in open position	accidents/ injuries	6,000
1990 Lexis	Cruise control may not dis- engage	accidents/ injuries	8,301
1984-88 Pontiac Fiero	Engine Fires	burns/deaths	244,000

TABLE 5.2 (CONTINUED)

RECENT RECALLS

Model Year/ Company	Reason Recalled	Potential Results	Number Sold
1986-1988 Volvo 740	Drive shaft may rub gas tank causing fire	accidents/burns/ deaths	38,000
1989 Ford Ranger 4 x 4 and Bronco II	Front wheel and hub may fall off	accidents/ injury	25,000
1991 Ford Explorer	Sunroofs may come off while vehicle moving	accidents/ injury	2,500
1989 Kawasaki ZX750	Handlebars may come off death	accidents/ injury/	1,953
1989 Coachman/ Viking Camping Trailers	Axle may come off	accident/ injury	486
Dynamic Classic Rowing Action Exerciser	spring may break	injury	2,000,000
Extra-Thick Super String Aerosol Party Streamers	Propellant may burn if sprayed near candles	burns	3,000,000
Century Infant Seat, 2000 STE	seat could fail	injury to infants/child	533,870

Adapted from *Consumer Reports Buying Guide* Issue for
1991 and individual *Consumer Reports* Issues, 1990 and 1991.

1.4 million Escorts over a three year period and not realize that the front seats had a tendency to come loose? Clearly, sometimes the actions which cause injury and death are more than accidents. Are recalls a fair, effective and safe way to deal with these behaviors? We will address the question of appropriate responses to corporate crime more fully in chapter 8.

With the issues of the effectiveness of recalls in mind, let us turn to an examination of vehicle safety, an area in which the recall has been widely used as a remedy for the production of unsafe products.

Vehicle Safety

One major area of consumer product safety regulation is automobile safety. In the 1960s, a revolution in assigning responsibility for auto injuries and deaths occurred. Previously, auto accidents were considered a matter of individual fault and were blamed on reckless, careless or inattentive drivers. Beginning in the 1960s, auto accidents began to be examined as a problem of engineering. In 1965, Ralph Nader argued that American automobiles could be designed to protect occupants in car crashes, but that auto companies were so concerned about styling that they were failing to design cars that were safe. Nader's (1965) assertions appear to be supported by Chrysler president Lee Iacocca's own phrase, "Safety doesn't sell" (Dowie 1977, 27). Nader argued, however, that the auto companies had a responsibility to build safer cars.

Nader attracted so much attention to his cause that Congress unanimously passed the Motor Vehicle Safety Act. This legislation gave the Department of Transportation (DOT) authority to write safety standards relating to automobile design and safety features. In addition, DOT could recall any car found to be unsafe. Since its inception, the National Highway Traffic Safety Administration has instituted regulations requiring lap-belts, collapsing steering columns, 5 mile-an-hour crash bumpers, and air bags/automatic seat belts, and has initiated the recall of automobiles and automotive products with unsafe designs (see examples in Table 5.2).

Consumer Product Safety

Another offspring of the Nader-initiated consumer move-ment is the Consumer Product Safety Commission. Created in 1972, this agency was authorized to recall any product found to be hazardous and to promulgate standards relating to the safe design of particular consumer products. Unfortunately, this Commission has been rather inactive, although it has estab-lished standards for flame-resistant children's sleepwear, child-resistant medicine bottle caps, the distance between slats in baby cribs, and safety features of lawnmowers and other con-sumer products (Clinard and Yeager 1980, 80).

Professional Services

A growing area of concern for consumer protection relates to the safety of professional services, particularly in the health care field. While professions such as medicine, nursing, and cosmetology have been subject to state licensing for many years, licensing boards have been ineffective in policing the professions.

In 1974 the Committee on Interstate and Foreign Commerce held hearings on unnecessary surgery. The final report summa-rizing the committee's findings estimated that 2.38 million unnecessary operations were performed in 1974 alone, result-ing in perhaps as many as 11,900 deaths (Stroman 1979, 7). Others (Reiman 1990, 65; Silver 1976) place the estimates higher: 3.2 million unnecessary operations and 15,000 deaths. Regardless, if patients (or surviving family members) discover that the surgery was unnecessary, a medical malpractice suit may be initiated. This private civil remedy provides some recourse for obtaining compensation, but probably is an inef-fective deterrent. While doctors' groups have been lobbying to limit medical malpractice claims, consumer groups have begun to press for more effective policing of the medical profession to eliminate unnecessary and incompetent surgery.

Reiman (1990, 65-66, 187) argues that unnecessary surgery is only the tip of the iceberg of corporate violence created by the medical profession, hospitals and the insurance industry.

Reiman estimates that between 6,000 and 32,000 people die each year from taking unnecessary prescription medicine (1990,187). To put these figures in perspective, Reiman compares the number of deaths from unnecessary surgery and unnecessary prescription medicines to the homicide rate—the crime of violence that law enforcement officials and the general public seem most concerned about. He discovered that the number of unnecessary medical deaths far outnumbered the number of homicides. Reiman (1990, 65) concluded that "[n]o matter how you slice it, the scalpel may be more dangerous than the switchblade," and that "the FBI should probably add the hypodermic needle and the prescription to their list of potential murder weapons."

WORKER HEALTH AND SAFETY

A second major area of health and safety regulation pertains to the workplace. Before the middle of the nineteenth century, safety at work was viewed as the responsibility of the worker. Workers were presumed to be aware of and to accept job risks as a normal aspect of employment. When accidents happened, workers were blamed for carelessness.

This situation began to change toward the end of the nineteenth century when states began to pass laws recognizing the inherent dangers of working with machinery and caustic substances. The laws that emerged established the employers' responsibility to safeguard workers against the worst hazards. These state laws were extremely weak, however, and were only sporadically enforced, if enforced at all.

The creation of worker compensation programs, in which injured workers were automatically compensated, placed some pressure on employers to reduce "lost-time accidents" and the incidence of "compensable" diseases because employers with a poor safety record were required to pay higher insurance premiums. Much progress in worker safety is attributable not to safety regulations but to the worker compensation insurance system.

During the 1960s, however, the continued existence of hazards in the workplace, particularly the growing problem of occupational diseases, gained prominence and resulted in the passage of a comprehensive federal program regulating these hazards and the creation of OSHA. Although the legislation provided a system for states to take over enforcement responsibilities for the federal agency, only about half of the states have opted to do so.

The OSHA Act provides criminal penalties only if an employer willfully violates an OSHA regulation by causing the death of an employee. All other violations are subject to civil penalties, even if the violation is willful. As might be expected, criminal penalties are rarely used because it is difficult to prove that the violation was willful and caused the death.

During its brief history, OSHA has come under heavy criticism (Calavita 1983; Donnelly 1982). Throughout the early 1970s, critics complained that OSHA was lax in enforcing significant violations of regulations, while at the same time being overly picky about violations that were essentially irrelevant to safety or health. In the later 1970s, OSHA's new regulations concerning chemicals and dust in the workplace were characterized by critics as being unreasonably strict and causing reduced productivity, increased inflation, and the decline of American industry in world markets.

Following the election of Ronald Reagan, OSHA's budget was slashed. Consequently, OSHA enforcement staff was greatly enfeebled, increasing the number of years—estimated to be 200 (Calavita 1983,439)—it would take to inspect every workplace in America. Further, during the Reagan years a number of proposed regulations were withdrawn, including one that required employers to inform employees of all toxic chemicals with which the employee had contact. Consistent with these changes, OSHA also sharply curtailed the number of cases it referred to the Justice Department for criminal prosecution (*Corporate Crime Reporter* 1987a, 13). In response to these changes, other critics have complained that OSHA has been captured by industry and is no longer a viable means of policing workplace hazards.

The prosecution of Film Recovery Systems and its executives (see Chapter 4) provides an example of a dramatic corporate crime of violence against workers, and the regulatory system's failure to protect workers. Typically, worker safety violations do not result in death or injury but present an increased risk of accident and injury. The hazards of exposure to potential carcinogens and mutagens are often unknown, and sometimes take many years to surface. Government regulations provide one means of protecting workers from these harms. Although we can never know which lives are saved, industrial safety experts know that protective regulations do save lives.

ENVIRONMENTAL PROTECTION

Historically, environmental protection was primarily a matter for conservationists who protected natural and recreational resources. Increasingly, however, environmental issues are being defined as health problems, and issues of public interest. For example, hazardous waste disposal, air pollution, and ground water contamination now pose significant health risks. Environmental catastrophes are a common occurrence. In recent years, whole cities have been evacuated because of chemical contamination. The 1984 disaster in Bhopal, India, in which 30,000 people were injured and more than 5,000 people died from fumes which escaped from a Union Carbide chemical plant, immediately brought a re-examination of environmental law and its enforcement (*Corporate Crime Reporter* 1987a, 5; 1988g, 11). People wanted to know whether the law would prevent a similar incident from occurring here (Lynch *et al.* 1989, 24). Only months after the Bhopal disaster, a chemical accident at one of Union Carbide's West Virginia plants injured 10 people and confirmed many people's worst fears (*New York Times* 1985, p. A1).

One problem is the law itself. Environmental law is a patchwork of overlapping statutes at various levels of government. Further, technology changes faster than the law, and creates new hazards even before existing hazards are understood and adequately controlled. As a result, the law seems to be playing catch-up, always one step behind the newest risk to health.

The most prominent agency in this network of enforcement

responsibility is the federal Environmental Protection Agency (EPA), which enforces environmental laws which contain both criminal and non-criminal provisions. Unquestionably, the EPA has an enormous job in monitoring pollution and correcting violations where they are found. It is a job made more difficult by firms that consciously evade the law.

The Story of Kepone:
A Case Study in Environmental Safety

A vivid example of an environmentally violent crime concerns Allied Chemical's production of Kepone, a highly toxic pesticide. Indeed, this story, related by Christopher Stone (1982), highlights the complex nature of these crimes as well as the limitations of the law in dealing with them (see also, Kelley 1981).

In the 1950s, Allied Chemical created Kepone, a new and highly toxic pesticide related to DDT, which caused kidney lesions, liver abnormalities, and nervous system damage in test animals. For several years, Allied Chemical licensed other manufacturers to produce Kepone, but in 1966, with demand for the chemical growing, Allied began to manufacture Kepone in its plant in Hopewell, Virginia.

Allied continued to produce Kepone until 1973, when two former employees of Allied started a new corporation, Life Sciences Products, Inc. (LSP), which acquired the sole rights to produce kepone. LSP began producing Kepone in March 1974 in a converted gas station in Hopewell, Virginia. The conditions in and around the plant were hardly a model of good environmental practices. According to the *Washington Star*, Kepone dust flew through the air, saturating everything and creating a dense cloud of dust around the factory. Within the first two weeks of production, workers at the factory began to experience "Kepone shakes." By the end of the second month of operation, bacterial digesters in the Hopewell sewage plant ceased to function, having been killed by Kepone in the sewage system.

About a year after the LSP plant began operations, a sick worker consulted his doctor about the symptoms he was experiencing. The doctor sent blood and urine samples to the Center for Disease Control (CDC). Specialists there found enough

Kepone in the blood sample to suspected that it had been accidentally contaminated. Nonetheless, the CDC's findings were sufficient to begin an investigation of LSP's work environment. As a result of the investigation, the LSP plant was shut down within a week.

Overall, the damage caused by Kepone was enormous, and the total damage is likely never to be known. At least 133 workers experienced symptoms of disease, including severe tremors, weight loss, liver tenderness, brain damage, chest pains, personality changes, eye flutters, and decreased ability to walk or stand. Significant quantities of Kepone were found in air samples taken sixteen miles from the plant, and water samples from sixty-four miles away. Forty people who did not work but *lived* in the vicinity, showed traces of Kepone in their blood. Restrictions on fishing were necessitated when Kepone was found in fish and oysters, costing the fishing and recreational industries from $4 to $24 million dollars. Nor is the damage over. Thousands of pounds of Kepone still lie on the river-bed, but it would cost $100 to $500 billion dollars to remove it through dredging, which would likely cause additional environmental violence.

Following the plant's closing, criminal charges were brought against LSP, Allied Chemical, and municipal officials. The two corporate officers of LSP were each charged with 153 violations of the federal Water Pollution Control Act, with potential penalties of $3.8 million dollars each. Both pleaded no contest, were fined $25,000 and placed on five years' probation. LSP, also charged with 153 violations, was fined $3.8 million dollars. By the time the penalty was imposed, however, the corporation was virtually dissolved and had no assets to pay the fine.

In addition, Allied Chemical was charged with aiding and abetting LSP in violating the Water Pollution Control Act. This charge was difficult to prove, and Allied was acquitted. However, Allied was charged and convicted of crimes stemming from its own misconduct in the production of Kepone from 1971 to 1974. Allied pleaded no contest to 940 counts of violating federal water pollution laws and was fined the maximum on each count, for a total of $13.24 million. This fine was reduced to $5 million when Allied agreed to "voluntarily" donate $8 million dollars to the Virginia Environmental Endowment and any other clean-up costs.

Although the criminal penalties in this case seem enormous, even a multimillion dollar fine is fairly easily absorbed by a corporation the size of Allied Chemical. As Christopher Stone (1982,288) noted, the fine was "spread over 28,500,000 shares of stock, as a non-recurring loss of about 33 cents a share...," meaning that stockholders, not the corporation itself, were punished. Further, the punishments were rather minor: no one went to jail or prison. From a conflict perspective, the Allied Chemical case stands as a further illustration of the relative immunity of corporations from punishment for their irresponsible and harmful acts.

The principal effect of criminal prosecution is the embarrassment and bad publicity the prosecution brings, and in the moral statement which it communicates to the public and other potential polluters. The unanswered question is whether all of these pains of prosecution are sufficient to deter those who might create dangerous pollution in the future.

Spreading the Blame

One final question is: Where were government watch-dogs while clouds of Kepone dust were literally swirling around the LSP factory? Why didn't the government do something more quickly to stop it? "The Virginia Air Quality Resources Board maintained an air-monitoring filter only a few hundred feet from the LSP plant. Unfortunately, Kepone was not among the list of things the station had been told to check on" (Stone 1982, 290). The Water Quality Control Board became aware of the Kepone problem in October 1974 and had the authority to shut down the plant, but decided to give LSP an opportunity to correct the problem voluntarily. OSHA and EPA investigators were also alerted to the problem in 1974 and 1975, but declined to actively investigate the situation.

One must wonder whether these government agencies share some moral responsibility for the illnesses resulting from the Kepone contamination. In this instance, one government body *was* held responsible. The City of Hopewell was fined $10,000 and given five years' probation for knowingly allowing Kepone to be dumped into the sewage system, the James River, and the air. Potentially, Hopewell could have been fined $3.9 million.

Since the early 1980s, criminal prosecution of corporations and corporate executives for environmental crimes has become more common, especially in relation to the manufacture, storage, handling and disposal of hazardous substances. Since 1983, the Environmental Crimes Section of the Department of Justice has brought indictments against 400 corporations, obtaining almost 300 convictions. In addition, individuals have served time in prison for violating environmental laws (*Corporate Crime Reporter* 1988h, 18).

CONCLUSION

Over the past twenty years, many new laws have been created which have defined certain risks as unacceptable. Although the agencies which are supposed to police these kinds of risks have frequently been criticized for lax enforcement, corporations and individuals have been prosecuted for violating health and safety laws where they could not have been prosecuted under more traditional criminal statutes. Under most of these new laws, there is no need to show that any actual harm has been done, or even that any risk of harm was actually produced. Instead, it is sufficient to show that a regulation, which has been designed to reduce the risk of certain harms, has been violated.

Critics of these new laws claim that the regulations seek to produce a "risk-free" world, which they claim is an impossible goal. Proponents of the new laws counter that the regulations seek to control only the most egregious risks, those which no rational person would voluntarily undertake. Other critics argue that the use of the criminal sanction in these instances is inappropriate because the acts which are addressed do not reflect public perceptions of "crime." Survey research tends to refute this point of view. Cullen *et al.* (1983, 483) found that eighty percent of respondents in their survey of attitudes about the seriousness of corporate and white-collar crime "stated that white-collar criminals have been treated too leniently, and deserve to be punished and incarcerated just as severely as 'regular street criminals.'"   Moreover, experimental research by Hans and Ermann (1989) suggests that people hold corporations to a "higher standard," are more likely to perceive corporations that behave recklessly as deserving more punishment than similarly reckless individuals, and are more likely to support criminal charges against corporations than against individuals who acted recklessly.

The law is both a reflection of social change and an instrument of change. As with all things that are new, resistance is to be expected. In the short time in which the new laws have existed, however, the level of acceptance is truly remarkable. While the corporate sector continues   to complain about the expense and burden of complying with regulations, the need for health and safety regulation is widely recognized. Similarly, while disputes continue regarding the proper use of the criminal sanction, strong support for the selective use of criminal sanctions for health and safety violations that offend community morality appears likely to continue.

Six

Green Crime: Corporate Violence and the Environment

THUS FAR WE have discussed a variety of violent crimes that corporations can commit. It should be clear by this point that corporate crimes of violence and the crimes that we traditionally associate with violence (i.e., street crimes like murder, rape and robbery), differ in several respects. One major difference concerns the degree and amount of harm inflicted by corporate criminals and street criminals. A second difference relates to the types of victims that are the focus of corporation violence.

As far as the type and amount of violence committed, corporations commit a wider variety of crimes that create much more violence than those perpetrated by individual street criminals (Reiman 1990). While individual street criminals prey upon other individuals via one-on-one crimes, corporate crimes tend to affect *masses* of individuals such as consumers and workers. This fact also justifies our focus on corporate violence. Each instance of corporate violence harms a large number of people.

The second difference, and the difference that this chapter shall investigate further, concerns the types of victims corporate crimes of violence affect. The victims of corporate crime are many, and include consumers, workers, and the general public. Corporate crimes of violence can also be directed at other entities that criminologists often fail to label as "victims." Specifically, corporate violence victimizes the environment, plant and animal life. In some respects, corporate acts of violence against the environment are "nontraditional" in the sense that they do not include a one-on-one harm, and they do not include human victims (although they might involve human victims as well as "green victims." See examples below). The nonhuman victims of corporate violence received greater attention from criminologists during the 1980s and 1990s, partially as the result of broad-based public environmental movements. Typically, however, criminologists have studied a limited segment of corporate acts of violence, primarily focusing upon environmental (e.g., pollution) or wildlife crimes (Mueller 1979).

Criminologists' interest in wildlife crimes stems from criminal laws designed to protect wildlife. However, the criminal law defines many wildlife crimes as crimes committed by individuals who, for example, hunt out of season or exceed a specified "bag" limit. Since our focus is on the corporation, we are concerned with a different type of environmental crime; crimes that are committed by corporate entities. In short, we will focus upon a variety of behaviors committed by organized groups who commit their violent crimes pursuing profit within the context of a legitimate business enterprise. Consequently, we are not concerned with wildlife crimes as traditionally defined in legal statutes since these crimes are committed by individuals.

Let us briefly address a second type of crime criminologists have studied: environmental crimes. Legally, environmental crimes include air, water and land pollution committed by individuals or corporations. Again, in this book we are not interested in the harmful acts individuals commit against the environment, but we are interested in acts of violence committed by corporate entities against the environment.

Generally, criminologists studying environmental crime adopt a traditional or legalistic approach. Consequently, they only study the behaviors that government officials are willing to recognize as harmful enough to be considered an environmental crime—or illegal behaviors defined by law. While a legalistic approach to environmental crime served to focus greater attention on the powerful's most serious environmental crimes, a strict legalistic approach also contains some severe limitations. The most serious of these limitations has to do with the creation of law and the extraordinary impact and control powerful corporations (through their lobbyists) can have on the structure of law. Since environmental law is often shaped by the powerful, environmental laws do not tend to completely represent the full extent, the nature and variety of crime the powerful can commit against the environment. In this chapter we wish to go beyond this narrow view of environmental crimes, and we will soon introduce a broader definition of crime that we will rely upon throughout this chapter. However, before we do so, it is necessary to make a few introductory comments about our position.

The crimes we will address in this chapter have no standard name, and we conceive of these crimes rather broadly. Many of the behaviors we will discuss are not currently defined as crimes, but are violent nevertheless. This chapter requires us to open our minds to the possibility that many behaviors not currently defined as criminal by law may be brought within the purview of the criminal law. This chapter thus deals with potential shifts in the moral boundary of crime.

The behaviors we will examine, while inclusive of crimes traditionally defined as environmental crimes (e.g. land, air and water pollution), eclipse this rather narrow definition of the environment. Consequently, in order to distinguish individual acts of violence against wildlife and the environment from massive corporate acts of violence against wildlife and the environment, we shall use the term "Green Crimes" (Lynch 1990).

What is a Green Crime?

To begin, green crimes are a specific type of corporate violence or a subset of all corporate crimes. Like corporate crimes, green crimes may or may not violate existing rules and regulations. Some are defined as criminal by law, others as civil, technical or administrative violations. Many of these acts of violence are not a violation of any existing form of law, even though they are violent enough or harmful enough that many argue that they should rightfully be treated as crimes (e.g. Lynch 1990; see also Schwendinger and Schwendinger 1970).

Green crimes come in a variety of forms. Some are quite familiar, for example, pollution and toxic chemical dumping. Other types of green crimes are less familiar, and take the form of timber clear cutting; capturing and importing rare and endangered animals for furs, pets and zoos; massive, cruel and unnecessary animal-experimentation for research purposes (a practice called vivisection); and selling unneeded and dangerous pesticides to Third World countries (drug and chemical dumping), farmers and homeowners. Some of these behaviors (e.g., chemical dumping) are promoted by corporations as methods of maintaining profits and escaping legal requirements imposed in their home country (Weir and Schapiro 1982; Lynch et al. 1988). Other behaviors (e.g., ivory trade, clear-cutting of timber, and illegal importation of animals) are linked to both consumer demands and corporate interests. In either case, corporations become involved in violent green crimes for the sake of profit.

There is an additional difference between green crimes and other environmental crimes. This difference has to do with the way in which green crimes are studied by criminologists. When we use the term green crime we are specifically implying a *value preference*. That preference, in short, is supported by a theoretical position which views green crimes in a political-economic context. In other words, the goal of green criminology is to analyze how political-economic factors are tied to the occurrence of corporate violence against the environment, animals, plants, etc. The idea is to connect corporate behavior and violence to economic forces.

Green Crimes of Violence: The Origin of an Idea

To many, it seems absurd to think of cutting down trees, capturing wild animals for research purposes or for sale as pets, or even the use of pesticides against bugs as violence. For centuries, this was part of everyday life. Before domestication of animals and the advent of the supermarket and clothing store, if we needed food or clothing we killed a wild animal. When we needed wood for the fireplace, or to build a home or make furniture, we cut down a tree. And, once humankind became more settled and developed agriculture, we killed bugs so that they would not harm our crops. When did people begin to think about these acts as crimes? And when did such behaviors begin to be recognized as violent behavior?

There have been various environmental movements throughout history which have affected the way we conceptualize the harms done to the environment, plants and animals (e.g., Theodore Roosevelt's "conservationist Movement," late 19th, early 20th century). The most extensive movements occurred in the 1960s. These movements began to depict many of society's excesses that harmed nature as violence. In the late 1980s, following decades of industrial pollution, oil-crises, and a growing list of endangered species, renewed interest in the environmental movement resurfaced. The idea that behavior like polluting, animal trapping, timber clear cutting, etc., were harmful generated what we now refer to as the green movement. This movement has broadened in recent years, and has even given rise to green political parties in a number of countries, including the U.S. (Postrel 1990; Walijassper 1990). In fact, the 1990s was originally dubbed the "Era of Environmentalism." In short, the tendency to view environmental harms as violence is a recent one.

This tendency, however, has become so influential in our society that many communities, organizations and corporations have established recycling programs to lessen some of the violence corporations commit against the environment. In fact, environmentalism has become so widespread in American culture that it has turned into a marketing ploy used by many corporations to sell their products. For example, some Barbie dolls now come with an "environmental consciousness," a piece of paper (hopefully recycled!) neatly tucked away in Barbie's packaging.

In more simple terms, the environmental movement of recent years has made many people aware that violence is not simply behavior that is directed against human beings—violence is any behavior which can be directed against living organisms that generates unnecessary pain, suffering and death. Sometimes this violence against nature has other repercussions, such as when migrant workers, consumers and even homeowners are poisoned by excessive use of dangerous pesticides. Thus, people too can be indirectly victimized when green crimes are committed.

As we noted above, the term green crimes implies that in thinking about crime, the theoretical frame of reference we will employ is based in political-economic theory. This connection between politics, economics and environmental harm is central to those subscribing to the "Green Politics Movement" (Postrel 1990, 58; Walijasper 1990, 59). Green political party members "view environmental destruction as an outcome of the structure of modern, industrialized capitalist production and consumption patterns" (Lynch 1990; see also, Sale 1990, 54). By taking this point of view, violent crimes against the environment can be analyzed as an outcome of: (1) how society is structured, both economically and politically, and (2) the structural pressures that are exerted upon corporations to make a profit.

Evidence of Green Violence

As we noted in chapter 1, the media is constantly bombarding us with unsettling facts about our environment and the violence against it. To give a few examples, did you know that over the past two decades, over 300 species of animals, birds, fish, reptiles, amphibians, snails, clams, crustaceans and insects have become extinct? That the Department of the Interior lists over 850 species (1100 species if plants are included) as endangered or threatened? And, did you know that this rate of extinction is unprecedented in the history of the world?

The Government's Role

Many argue that this violent destruction of the environment is largely due to the behavior of corporations (Sale 1990). Often times, however, such behaviors are sanctioned by the government and, in some cases, actually promoted by the government.

Frequently, governmental public policies of a few decades ago are the problem. Outdated and ill-conceived public policies have, it seems, become today's environmental nightmare. For instance, during the 1930s, the federal government funded a massive program of hydroelectric dam construction on the Columbia River in Washington and Oregon. Until recently, these projects were hailed as success stories. The federal government and utility companies that generate electricity through these dams pointed proudly to the clean and cheap electricity produced by the dams. However, it has become clear that the dams are the major cause of the rapidly decreasing numbers of salmon in the Pacific Northwest. The dams interfere with the ability of the salmon to spawn upstream and successfully return to the sea. Some species of salmon are now near extinction, and others are quickly becoming endangered.

Despite a growing understanding of the causes of the problems for the salmon, the solutions are less clear. Should the dams be ripped down to save some fish? What about the people who live in this area? An entire economy, dependent on cheap electric power, has grown up in the region. For example, a number of aluminum smelting plants have been built in this area because of their heavy electrical demands. Tens of thousands of workers are employed in these plants. Public policy appears to be deadlocked on the issue. Some species of salmon, however, may not survive until a solution is found.

This and many other examples point out the difficulties of "drawing lines." Clearly, the law does not make the actions of the hydroelectric operators criminal or illegal. Should it be a crime? Should the violence associated with destroying an entire species of fish be allowed to continue? How should the interests of salmon fishermen be weighed against the interests of industrial workers? How should the interests of the salmon itself be weighed against the interests of humans? We will return to similar questions in the remaining chapters that address appropriate responses to corporate violence.

Pesticides and Green Crime

Other examples of "green crimes," though they involve no violation of the law, present somewhat less ambiguous moral problems. Quite recently, numerous stories concerning corporations that "make our lawns healthy and green" (involving both the companies that produce and apply chemicals to our lawns) have occupied much media space. These exposés have unearthed evidence that overuse of common lawn care products (e.g., fertilizers, herbicides and pesticides) have damaged the environment and drinking water supplies in many neighborhoods, causing thousands of severe illnesses and life-threatening allergic reactions, and even death. Should keeping your lawn green be a crime? That depends upon how we look at the situation and how the behavior of chemical companies is interpreted (e.g., Rabinovitch 1981; Epstein 1979). Let us provide some information that might help make this decision.

Most companies that sell pesticides suggest "treatment schedules" for a "well maintained lawn that you can be proud of," or to maintain healthy crops. Pesticide manufactures also "impose" similar treatment schedules on poor Third World farmers and plantation owners in order to sell more of their product (Weir and Schapiro 1982). A treatment schedule tells you how much and when to apply a particular pesticide to your lawn or crops. Typically, these schedules suggest treatments even when your lawn or crops are healthy. Chemical manufacturers argue that treating healthy lawns and crops is a necessary preventive measure. The problem is that corporations that employ pesticide application schedules promote excessive consumption of pesticides, insure that "pests" establish immunity to the pesticides (and consequently requires the development, marketing and application of more potent pesticides to kill off immune pests), and damage the health of farm workers, consumers and the environment. In recent years, a growing number of Americans have developed sensitivities to many of the lawn chemicals commonly used by their neighbors and lawn care companies. Some people are so badly affected by these products that they must wear air-tight body suits in order to leave their homes.

Numerous pesticide and lawn product manufactures and lawn care companies also use known carcinogens in their products. Many of these "component chemicals" used in pesticides were placed on the market over three decades ago with little or no scientific testing, at a time when governmental regulations were less strict than they are today. The environmental harm these products create and the human suffering they generate are enormous. Should such activities be allowed to continue? Should they be outlawed? These questions are growing moral dilemmas that the law will soon address.

You should get the picture by now: many activities that we consider normal have detrimental environmental consequences. And, even though we know about the harms that are generated, companies continue to produce hazardous chemicals, and people continue to use them. These observations lead to a simple conclusion: Green crimes are very widespread. Where do corporations commit these crimes? All around you—even in your own backyard!

Green Crimes and the Third World

Green crimes are not limited to your backyard: they occur worldwide and are promoted as "good business" by many major American corporations (e.g. Hinds 1982; Silverman *et al.* 1982). In their book, *Circle of Poison*, Weir and Schapiro describe the international trade in pesticide, revealing some alarming facts, and naming such major corporations as "Dow, Shell, Stauffer, Chevron, Ciba-Geigy...Bayer, Monsanto, ICI, Dupont,...Hooker,... Allied...[and] Union Carbide..." as participants (1982,4). At the time they were researching their book, Weir and Schapiro found that 25 percent of pesticides exported from the U.S. were banned, restricted or unregistered for use in the U.S. because of the hazards they posed (1982, 4). A decade later, the U.S. has still failed to take steps that would make the export of banned and unregistered chemicals illegal (a practice commonly called "dumping"). In fact, some researchers claim that the problem of exporting dangerous, banned, unregistered chemicals to foreign nations has worsened under both the Reagan and Bush administrations (Scanlan 1991a, 1991b). Legislation to stop the sale of banned and unregistered chemicals to foreign nations was defeated in Congress in 1990 (Scanlan 1991a, 5a). Consequently, a company like DowElanco, a major pesticide manufacturer, cannot sell one of its herbicides, Galant, in the U.S. because the EPA has restricted its sale in the U.S. as a suspected carcinogen (Scanlan 1991a, 1a). Yet, DowElanco *may* (and does) sell Galant, unrestricted to other nations like Costa Rica. The fact that no laws exist to stop this practice does not make this behavior any less harmful, reprehensible or unethical. And, while such behavior is certainly unethical, a more damning criticism can be made of such practices. This argument suggests that companies which sell banned chemicals to other nations, particularly Third World nations, are involved in a racial form of genocide and are participating in racist marketing practices.

To make matters worse, the chemical and drug dumping scandal itself is just the tip of the iceberg. Not only are dangerous chemicals, which are banned from sale in the U.S., freely exported to Third World countries, they are often used in ways that make them even more dangerous than they already are. As Weir and Schapiro explain:

> In Third World countries...[w]orkers are seldom told how...pesticides can hurt them. Most cannot read. And even if they could, labels on banned pesticides often do not carry...warnings...[and are f]requently... simply scooped out..., handled like harmless white powder by peasants who have little experience with manmade poisons (p.7).

> Some farmworkers try to wash the pesticide from their skin...us[ing] the [water from] irrigation ditches, laced with...toxic runoff of insecticides, thereby compounding their contamination (p.13).

In poor Third World countries, peasants use unlabeled plastic pesticide liners as raincoats (p.15), or pesticide drums that are unlabeled, or labeled in a foreign language—English—as water collection barrels.

Furthermore, there is a "boomerang effect" in this international pesticide trade or "circle of poison" (Weir and Schapiro 1982, 28-30). Many of the banned pesticides that American corporations ship overseas for use on foreign crops are reimported to the U.S. on the foods that we eat! Thus, corporations who escape U.S. regulations designed to safeguard people and the environment by shipping banned pesticides to foreign markets create violence in Third World nations and here in the U.S.

A Clear Cut Case of Green Crime

Another fast growing green crime in the news recently is the clear cut. Motivated by huge profits in the hardwood timber and paper industries, many corporations are devastating the world's pristine and last remaining rainforests to market wood products, containers, etc. (Mardon 1991; Connelley 1991; DeBonis 1991; Rauber 1991; Barry 1991; Rainforest Action Network 1990 a,b,c,d,e). Rainforests necessary to the world's ecosystem, which have taken thousands of years to develop, are being lost in the process. Deforestation contributes to the greenhouse effect and the extinction of plants, animals and insects worldwide. This violence may eventually affect humans, as global temperatures rise, coastal flooding occurs, pollution and respiratory illnesses increase, and the planet's natural balance is thrown off kilter.

But again, corporations are not solely to blame for this problem. As noted above, sometimes governmental policies contribute to the types of green crime corporations commit. A recent example is found in the timber industry, where the federal government is selling off millions of acres of national park land and timber to private logging firms, and in the process destroying the natural habitat of many wildlife species (DeBonis 1991). The government is not doing this for profit, but to create a profitable environment for the timber industry.

Animal Experimentation

Another way in which large corporations commit green violence is through animal experimentation (American Anti-Vivisection Society 1989; Kaufman 1989; Goodall 1989; Goldberg and Frazier 1989; Seigel 1989; *Health and Humane Research* 1991), or by using animals to test for the harmful effects of various product. Many may object the idea that animal experimentation is violence—unnecessary violence—committed by corporations. Certainly, testing products on animals is necessary to protect humans from the types of corporate violence described in previous chapters. Or is it? Unfortunately, these experiments are often gruesome (Pacheco 1991), unnecessary and questionable in terms of saving human lives (Seigel 1989; Health and Humane Research 1991). For example, Leslie Fain, an employee at Gillette, recently gave this account of the environment at a Gillette Laboratory during some of the testing rituals:

> Technicians laughed while they put FOAMY SHAVING CREAM and LIQUID PAPER in [test] rabbit's eyes and callously force-fed RIGHT GUARD deodorant to animals in death tests (Pacheco 1991, 1).

Gillette is not alone; most products commonly available in your local store are tested on animals in similar or more horrid fashions by companies like Proctor and Gamble, Bristol-Myers and Cosmair (Pacheo 1991, 1; see Table 7.1 for a list of Common Household Products Tested on Animals). In certain cosmetic tests, for example, rabbits have their heads placed in restraining devices and their eyelids removed so that cosmetic companies can test their products on eye tissue. The rabbit also has a large collar placed around its head so that it cannot scratch or rub its eyes. The eyelids are removed so the rabbit's eye's do not water and expel the irritating chemical purposely placed there.

Are these types of tests and the violence they generate necessary to human health and safety? Are they effective means of keeping people safe? How do we weigh the rights of animals against the rights of people?

According to Alex Pacheco (1991: 3), "100 million animals

TABLE 7.1
SAMPLE OF COMMON HOUSEHOLD PRODUCTS TESTED ON ANIMALS

Banner	Downy	Pringles
Bold	Duncan Hines	Puffs
Bounce	ERA	Puritan Oil
Bounty	Folgers	Safeguard
Biz	Gleem	Scope
Camay	Head & Shoulders	Secret
Cascade	Ivory	Spic and Span
Charmin	Jif	Sunny Delight
Cheer	Lincoln Products	Sure
Citrus Hill	Luvs	Texsun Products
Clearasil	Mr. Clean	Tide
Coast	Norwich Asprin	Top Job
Comet	Oil of Olay	Vicks Cough & Cold
Crest	Pampers	Vidall Sassoon
Crisco	Pepto-Bismol	Winter Hill
Dawn	Pert	Zest

(Adapted from Publications by PETA, 1990-1991, Product Name Alphabetized)

die agonizing deaths from experiments every year, with nearly 20 million of these deaths from cosmetics and household product testing...." Yet many of these products remain unsafe, or contain carcinogens and poisons. Further, it is unclear whether these violent animal tests are even appropriate (Seigel 1989). For instance, a chemical that does not cause cancer in rats or rabbits may cause cancer in humans given the genetic and anatomical differences between human and animal species (for a different view, see Epstein 1979). If such animal testing were the only way of protecting humans, it would be a necessary evil. The simple fact is that this type of corporate violence is *not necessary* given the types of medical technology available today (Goldberg and Frazier 1989; and discussion below). Moreover, animal tests are frequently less efficient than alternative methods such as testing products on human skin cultures (Goldberg

and Frazier 1989; and discussion below; for a list of products
not tested on animals and containing no animal by-products see
Table 7.2). Such alternatives are not widely used, however,
simply because to be less violent, corporations would have to
spend more money to employ skin culture tests or because
corporations believe that government regulatory agencies will
be more easily convinced of the safety of the product if animal
tests are used. In this corporate cost-benefit equation, innocent
animals continually lose out to the corporate balance sheet.

This behavior is not only violence, it is BIG business.
Estimates of the number of animals employed in U.S. laboratories, the majority by corporations, range from 10 to 100 million
per year (*Health and Humane Research* 1991, 5). As noted in
Health and Humane Research:

> Predictably, there has been a fierce backlash [against
> banning animal experimentation] from those whose profits
> and livelihood depend on the survival of vivisection....
> Industry and pro-animal research organizations have
> mounted aggressive...well funded [corporate] campaigns to
> discredit opponents [of animal experimentation]. [These
> organizations have]...used emotional blackmail...preying on
> the fear of disease to sustain public acceptance of animal
> sacrifices (1991, 2).

But, the claims made by the laboratory animal industry are
largely false. Two factors are worth mentioning.

First, as we implied above, because the physiological differences between humans and animals are so great, substances
which have no effect in animals may affect humans. This is
because substances are metabolized differently in humans and
in animals (*Health and Humane Research* 1991, 10). For instance, "cortisone produces birth defects in mice, but not in
people, while thalidomide works the other way around" (*Health
and Humane Research* 1991,10). Encainide and Flecanide, approved following animal experiments, have been responsible
for over 300 deaths in humans (Altman 1987). Over fifty percent
of all drugs approved by the FDA between 1976 and 1985 on the
basis of animal experimentation were later found to cause

TABLE 7.2
SAMPLE OF COMPANIES THAT DO NOT TEST THEIR
PRODUCTS ON ANIMALS*

A Clear Alternative	Home Service Product Company
Amberwood	JLM Enterprises
American Cosmetic	Key West Fragrances/Cosmetics
Aroma Vero Company	KSA-Jojoba
Aura Cacia	Manufacturing LabsKMS
Belvedere Labs	M&N Natural Products
Bioskosma	Microbalanced Products
Campana Corporation	Natural Organics
Comfort Manufacturing Company	Natural Brand Cosmetics
Community Soap Factory	New World Minerals
Compassion Cosmetics	Paul Penders, USA
Dr. F.H. Bronner	PETA
Essentials	I. Rokeach & Sons
Golden Lotus	Sirena Tropical Soap Company
Granny's Old Fashion	Sleepy Hollow Natural Products
Products	Vegan Street

*The sample chosen for this Table reflects companies that (1) do not test
on animals and (2) use no animal by-products or ingredients in their
products. Adapted From PETA Newsletters (1991).

serious illness, injury and death in humans (FDA Drug Review
1990). Numerous animal test on tobacco smoke have failed to
induce cancer in animals. Consequently, people were not warned
about the dangers of smoking until recently (*Health and Humane Research* 1990, 11). Even Pfizer, one of the nations largest
drug manufacturers, has recognized the deficiencies in, yet still
uses, animals to test the effect of drugs. Pfizer's own research
on the effects of cancer causing substances in humans, rats and
mice indicates that in most cases "the animal test had given the
wrong answer" (*Health and Humane Research* 1990, 9; Salsburg
1983, 63-67).

The second important point is that animal experiments are
not the most effective means of testing drugs and chemicals—

simply the cheapest. Widely available alternatives to animal testing provide much more accurate results. These alternatives include human tissue testing, computer simulation and clinical studies.

Alternatives to the Crime of Animal Testing

Testing drugs and chemicals directly on human tissue samples (in vitro experimentation) appears to be the most accurate test. Human cells from different organs can be easily grown in laboratories and used in place of animals. There is no suffering, and no sacrificing of life in this procedure. One reason this method is not more widely used is that it costs more than mice or rats. And, even though the results of in vitro experimentation are more accurate, cost remains the "bottom line." Corporations cannot take all the blame here, however. In certain instances, governmental agencies require that tests be performed on animals before the agency will approve a substance for sale to the general public. Thus, to some degree, a change in public policy is required to remedy this situation.

An increasingly popular alternative to animal testing is computer simulation. Computers can be programmed to respond just as the human body would to the introduction of drugs and chemicals into a simulated human system. While this idea seems far-fetched, experiments demonstrate that computer simulation techniques are more accurate than animal experimentation (*Health and Humane Research* 1991, 14). In England, the use of animals in medical schools has been outlawed and replaced by a computer simulation technique called "biovideograph." Biovideographs are used to practice surgical techniques and have been found to be more effective than animal surgical practice in turning out better trained surgeons (*Heath and Humane Research* 1991, 18).

A final alternative, one more widely used to study disease transmission earlier in this century, is the clinical study. Clinical studies examine people who have already contracted a disease and attempt to determine the cause of the disease so that it may be prevented in the future. Clinical studies have been responsible for more medical advances than animal experimentation (*Health and Humane Research* 1991, 2).

The main reason the medical profession and chemical and drug companies continue to rely upon animal experimentation is that our view of disease is outdated. We continue to rely upon the use of animal experimentation in an attempt to reverse the effects of disease, when we know that most diseases are related to environmental factors, nutritional habits and social class (*Health and Humane Research* 1991, 7). The Center for Disease Control estimates that 70 percent of the leading disease causes of death are related to lifestyle and environmental factors (*Health and Humane Research* 1991, 8). Much disease can be prevented, and the way to fight disease is not through animal experimentation but through education and environmental programs.

In short, the pain and suffering—the violence—associated both directly (through pain inducing experiments) and indirectly (through massive, cruel and unhealthy animal breeding program, and human deaths) with animal experimentation is unnecessary. As the researchers for *Health and Humane Research* concluded, vivisection is not only in error, it is morally questionable (p. 11), meaning that the use of animal experimentation "must be regarded as *bad science*" (p. 20, emphasis added).

Conclusion

The pain inflicted upon animals—part of the environment—is endless. We could continue with the gruesome details, for the list goes on and on and on.... The killing of dolphins by large tuna fishery companies; the clubbing of baby seals for fur coats; the inhumane slaughtering of cattle and chickens; the force-feeding and raising of baby cows (veal) in dark confinement in small steel holding cells, etc. The point should be clear: corporate violence is everywhere; even harmless animals are its victims.

Corporations have victimized the environment, animals, and plants for a century and more without anyone questioning their violent tactics. A social movement to end this violence emerged in the 1960s and 1970s, and has only recently become

a force for corporate America to reckon with. This chapter has
exposed readers to only a few of the green crimes corporations
commit. This brief review is designed to make this type of
activity more visible and to bring this behavior into the fold of
concerns criminologists deal with as crime. We hope that
criminologists pay more attention to these types of harms in
the future, and that when addressing corporate crime they do
not fail to address the violence directed at mother nature and
all its creatures, from the biggest to the smallest.

Clearly, societal values and a moral vocabulary are only now
beginning to take shape. The Green Movement challenges many
long-held and cherished presumptions. This chapter has intentionally blurred the moral boundaries of crime to demonstrate
the difficulty in deciding what types of activities should be
criminal and what policies should be developed to deal with the
problem. It may not, for example, be wise or necessary to deal
with some of the behavior mentioned in this chapter through
the criminal justice system. Other remedies, which will be
discussed in the following chapters, may be more appropriate.

Moreover, where "green" is at issue, it is more difficult for
us to point a finger of blame at "those evil corporations."
Corporations cannot take all the blame; and consumers and the
government (through its public policy decisions) also contribute to green crimes. Consumers find themselves employing
many of the same neutralizations that corporate executives do
in justifying our continued use of products that endanger the
environment or specific species. It becomes more and more
difficult for us to distinguish between rationalizations and
valid justifications. To make this distinction at all, however,
requires that we recognize our own "blind spots" regarding
corporate violence.

Seven

Explaining Corporate Crime

THE MOST SIMPLISTIC and common explanation of the causes of corporate violence is profit. That is, corporations cut corners on safety and health issues—manufacturing faulty products, allowing dangerous working conditions to persist, or fouling the environment—for the sake of protecting or improving their profitability. Clearly, the bottom line matters to corporate executives (Jackall 1988), but a full understanding of the causes of corporate violence requires a more sophisticated approach.

Criminologists have offered a number of explanations besides the profit motive to explain the origins of corporate violence. These explanations examine the psychological characteristics of corporate criminals (Reckless 1973), subcultural corporate processes through which executives learn to give health, safety and environmental concerns a low priority (Sutherland 1949), and organizational factors, such as industrial concentration or the goals of stability, prestige, and growth (Finney and Lesieur 1982; Barnett 1981; Clinard and Yeager 1980, 48). Below, we take a further look at these explanations.

Before we get down to reviewing these theories, let us briefly examine the elements a "good" theory of crime should examine, and discuss two different types of theory used to explain corporate crime: micro (subjective) and macro (structural) theory.

EXPLAINING CRIME WITH "GOOD THEORY"

In explaining crime, criminologists (and others) employ observations, statistics and even conjecture to develop a logical theory of crime. Whatever perspective the theorist chooses as the basis of the theoretical explanation (e.g., biological, sociological, economic, etc.), a theory of crime needs to address three issues in order to be considered adequate: motivation, opportunity, and law enforcement/social control. Each of these issues raises a different set of questions.

Questions regarding motivation include: Why do people commit crime? What motivates people to deviate? Do criminals possess different characteristics than non-criminals? Are criminals and non-criminals found in different social contexts that generate different motivations to commit crime? Opportunity considerations generate questions such as: Can all people commit corporate violence? Or are there opportunity factors, such as class-location which provide access to criminal means and make some people more likely than others to commit corporate violence? Finally, there are social control and law enforcement questions to address: Are the behaviors being examined currently defined as crimes? Are there legal mechanisms and social control organizations to detect and punish these behaviors? Is there a class-bias built into the focus of formal social control? Questions related to law and social control also involve questions of deterrence and the personal or social circumstances that bond one to society in a way that controls the individual's (or corporation's) behavior (e.g. Hirschi 1969).

LEVELS OF ANALYSIS

There are numerous decisions to make when constructing a good theory. First, we must make a choice between disciplines (e.g., sociological, psychological, biological explanations) or pick a discipline with which to begin. This has an effect on a second decision we must make: at what level of analysis will our theory will be pitched? The macro or micro-level?.

Macrolevel or *structural explanations* address the role of sociological or economic factors—such as social structure, culture, class structure and membership, and type of economic organization—in affecting motivations, opportunities, bonding and social control functions. Within corporate crime research, *modified macrolevel analyses* examine the more immediate structural context and origins of crime, specifying how organizational structures (the corporate context) affect criminality (e.g., see Jackall 1988).

Historically, the most prevalent approach for explaining crime emphasizes *microlevel*, situational, *subjective* or *individual-level* factors that cause crime, such as IQ, the psychological make-up of offenders, or the individual's biological predisposition toward crime. Microlevel theory attempts to: (1) identify the personal characteristics of criminals and (2) demonstrate that these characteristics differ from those possessed by non-criminals.

Typically, criminologists tend to opt for one level of analysis to the exclusion of the other. For example, a psychologically-oriented criminologist will examine the individual characteristics of criminals, without considering how macro-sociological factors may influence psychological development and adjustment. Recently, however, many criminologists have argued in favor of integrating structural and subjective theories (e.g., Groves and Lynch 1990). While this approach has only recently been of concern to many criminologists, corporate researchers have already taken this issue to heart and have demonstrated a connection between macro- and micro-level concerns. Clinard and Yeager (1980, 44-45), for instance, argue that: "Lower level personnel receive directives from above about desired goals, be they production quotas or development of a new product. These goals can easily be seen as absolute requirements...." Lower level managers interpret their own paths to career advancement within the goals set forth by corporate management, which are, in turn, affected by economic conditions and other market forces.

But why integrate macro and micro theory? The answer is simple: integrating or connecting these two levels of analysis allows both subjective and structural levels to come together in a way that provides a much richer explanation of crime (Groves and Lynch 1990). Be that as it may, criminologists must still select either the macro or micro level of analysis as a starting point for theory building, even when integration is the goal.

A "good theory" of corporate violence will, therefore, be an "integrated theory." As such, it must address the following question: how do macro and micro level motivations, opportunities and social control intersect to produce corporate crime? We will return to a further consideration of an integrated theory of corporate crime. But first, let us review several micro and macro-level explanations of corporate crime that will provide some of the raw materials for an integrated view.

CORPORATE CRIME: MICRO-LEVEL EXPLANATIONS

A number of theorists have used microlevel theory to discuss the causes of corporate crime. These theories consider subjective factors such as the biological and psychological development of corporate criminals, as well as psychological rationalizations they use to justify corporate violence and appease their consciences.

Psychological and Biological Explanations

Several researchers have addressed the individual factors that they believe contribute to corporate and white-collar crime. Jeffrey (1990), for example, argues that an individual's IQ affects their ability to learn complicated techniques used to commit corporate crimes. His general theory of crime argues that certain people may be predisposed by their biological and neurological make-up to commit crime, corporate crime included. In his research, Reckless (1973) suggests that white-collar offenders may indeed be predisposed to commit crime, and concluded that many found it difficult to resist the temptations presented by their crimes, and lacked appropriate inner-control mechanisms.

A preference for individualistic explanations is also found in views which argue that people who commit corporate crimes do so because crime is more rewarding or pleasurable for them than conformity (Hirschi and Gottfredson 1987; Jeffrey 1990, 340). In other words, corporate crime, like street crime, can be viewed as a rational choice (Box 1983, 43). Each individual offender weighs the costs and rewards associated with conformity and deviance, calculating which alternative nets them a greater gain. To some extent, this view implies that corporate offenders' personalities may be related to their criminal behavior.

In his review of the literature on the connection between personality and corporate crime, Coleman (1985, 195-197) argues that two characteristics stand out among elite criminals: they are egocentric and reckless (see also: Bromberg 1965; Blum 1972). In other words, these individuals are willing to take chances to benefit themselves, and one of the chances they might be willing to take is crime. Along similar lines, Steven Box (1983, 37-43) has argued that corporations attract and select people with personality characteristics that make crime a likely outcome. Box notes that corporations sometimes bring in "cunning people" to do their dirty work and that those who "rise to the top" in a corporation "are likely to have just those personal characteristics it takes to commit corporate crime...." (1983,39). The characteristics which make a person successful in the business world and which in turn may lead to crime, are reinforced by the nature of the corporate organization and "by the psychological consequences of success itself...." (Box 1983,39).

There is much more literature suggesting the individualistic nature of corporate crime. But, there has been very little concrete research about individuals who commit corporate crimes. As C. Ray Jeffrey (1990, 339)—a prominent supporter of the bio-psychological perspective—notes: "There have been no major studies of the biological and psychological make-up of white-collar criminals, and we certainly do not know the bio-chemical and neurological functioning of these persons" (see also Balkan *et al.* 1980, 174). Jeffrey prefers to view these crimes (and all crimes) as the result of a complex interaction between past learning and experiences, the environment, and the brain's interpretation of what is or is not pleasurable (stimuli). In his view, the latter neurological function dominates the process.

Neutralizing a Nagging Conscience

A fairly large number of researchers has found that corporate executives employ certain rationalizations to "neutralize" their consciences. By neutralizing one's conscience, a corporate executive can continue to ignore the violence being perpetrated. Thus, there is evidence that psychological process may have an impact upon the commission of corporate violence. Much of the research into this psychological aspect of corporate crime is based upon Sykes and Matza's *techniques of neutralization* theory (e.g., Conklin 1977; Benson 1985; Coleman 1985, 206-212; Cressey 1971; and Box 1983). Sykes and Matza's theory was specifically designed to examine ways in which juvenile delinquents use techniques of neutralization to absolve themselves of blame and redefine their criminal acts as justifiable. These techniques are rationalizations that assuage guilt. Similar techniques are observed in the context of corporate crimes of violence (e.g., Benson 1985; Coleman 1985, 206-212; Box 1983, 54-57; Jackall 1988).

Like juvenile delinquents, corporate managers who know that things are "not being done right" use a variety of techniques for neutralizing their consciences. As their conscience is put at rest, they decrease their efforts to correct the problem. Some rely upon these rationalizations before or after the fact to justify their plan of action. These rationalizations are learned, either by trial-and-error or through the example of others in a specific historical and institutional context (Benson 1985, 588). Among the neutralizations corporate officials use are denial of injury, denial of evil, denial of the victim, condemnation of the condemners and the appeal to higher loyalties. We briefly review these techniques of neutralization below.

Denial of the Injury. The Ford Pinto case provides a classic injury denial rationalization: accidents will happen, and automobile accidents will often kill people. Ford argued that they did not create the injury; they simply manufactured a car. This rationalization suggests that death is, in short, part of the risk people assume when they buy and drive cars.

Denial of Evil. A similar neutralization is to deny any wrongdoing or responsibility. For example, after reading aloud the definition of fraud from an engineer's handbook, a senior engineer at B.F. Goodrich involved in fraudulent reporting of aircraft brake tests claimed that "...I don't think what we're doing can be called fraud" (Vandivier 1982, 115, 119). The engineer's supervisor argued that false test reports were not "really lying. All we were doing was interpreting figures the way we knew they should be. We were just exercising some engineering license" (Vandivier 1982).

Another common version of this rationalization involves the claim: "everyone does it." Thus, a person's guilty conscience about dumping small quantities of a toxic chemical into the river may be neutralized by asserting that all companies do it. And, if everyone does it—if dumping is a common industry practice—how could it be wrong?

Denial of the Victim. This neutralization technique places the blame on the victim or denies that a real person was actually hurt by the faulty product (Box 1983, 55-56). The victim may also be seen as "getting what they deserved." For example, some corporate executives believe that workers who get cancer are biologically predisposed to cancer and would have gotten cancer regardless of how their work environment was structured. Many of the people who claim they got lung cancer from asbestos also smoked cigarettes, so why blame the asbestos? In the automotive industry, a similar view is held of automobile accidents: most accidents are caused by "the nut behind the wheel" rather than by defective automobile design.

A similar tactic is to minimize the extent of the harm by comparing it to some other, more prevalent harm. For example, the defendants in the Film Recovery Systems case (see Chapter 4) may have told themselves that illegal aliens are "lucky to have a job," so that, compared to the life they would lead back in their own country—unemployed, living at subsistence level—they are far better off, even when health and safety is at risk. Corporate executives responsible for dumping banned products overseas also cling to the belief that Third World farmers are better off with dangerous pesticides than with no pesticides at all. How else could they feed their hungry populations? (see Weir and Shapiro 1985).

Condemnation of Condemners. This rationalization works through a process that attempts to reverse the imputation of guilt. In other words, corporate criminals might place the blame for their illegal and harmful behavior on the government or on regulations that they view as overly strict. Using this neutralization technique, corporate officials deny the legitimacy of law, claim that certain laws are unnecessary, and that laws which interfere with corporate enterprises are a restriction of the free-market ethic of American capitalism (Box 1983, 56-57). In short, corporate officials reverse the blame and make regulation and regulatory officials into the "real bad guys."

Appeal to Higher Loyalties. This technique takes many forms, some ideological and others more concrete. One common form of this neutralization is to insist that management has a responsibility to the stockholders to maximize profits. It is the government's, not the company's, job to look after safety and health. This neutralization has been given the garb of scientific legitimacy in the writings of Milton Friedman (Stone 1975, 75) who notes that "Few trends could so thoroughly undermine the very foundations of our free society as the acceptance of a social responsibility other than to make as much money for their stockholders as possible" (Friedman 1962, 133).

Another appeal to higher loyalties utilizes cost-benefit analysis. Here corporations examine the costs required to protect consumers and the general public from injury and conclude that unless the benefits outweigh the costs, it is inappropriate to take that precaution. As discussed earlier, this strategy was used by the Ford Motor Company in relation to the Pinto gas tank (Dowie 1977, 24; see chapter 4).

In other cases, the higher loyalties are less abstract and strike closer to home. When employees of B.F. Goodrich were being told to falsify qualification reports on a new aircraft brake, they were faced with an ethical choice. Personal responsibilities to their families frequently overshadowed moral responsibilities. Vandivier (1982, 112) recalls the dilemma faced by one of his colleagues at Goodrich who was ordered by managers to falsify an engineering report.

> "You know," he went on uncertainly, looking down at his desk, "I've been an engineer for a long time, and I've always believed that ethics and integrity were every bit as important as theorems and formulas, and never once has anything happened to change my beliefs. Now this.... Hell, I've got two sons I've got to put through school and I just..." His voice trailed off.
>
> He sat for a few more minutes, then, looking over the top of his glasses, said hoarsely, "Well, it looks like we're licked. The way it stands now, we're going to go ahead and prepare the data and other things for the graphic presentation in the report, and when we're finished, someone upstairs will actually write the report."

Frequently these appeals are based upon elevating business ethics and practices above the law. Box (1983, 57) has argued that this technique of neutralization is "embedded in the 'structural immorality' of corporations." Jackall (1988) makes a similar observation, noting that expediency is the reigning value in corporate decision-making. The ability to fashion workable rationalizations is one of the marks of an organizationally valuable employee—that is, one who will be rewarded and promoted. As one executive remarked, "We have to support each other and we have to support the hierarchy. Otherwise you have no management system" (Jackall 1988, 132).

Denial of responsibility. Probably the most common neutral-ization technique is to deny personal responsibility (e.g., "I wasn't really sure that anything was wrong. It's someone else's job to attend to health and safety concerns"). Vandivier (1982, 113) reports that a superior asked to inform the chief engineer of false test reports responded that it was none of his business: "I learned a long time ago not to worry about things over which I have no control. I have no control over this." Vandivier asked the superior how he would feel if a pilot were injured or killed during a test-flight: "Look," he [the superior] said, becoming somewhat exasperated, "I just told you I have no control over this thing. Why should my conscience bother me?"

The motivation for applying any of these neutralizations comes from the organizational members' *unwillingness* to frustrate the goals of the organization. The person wants to be a team player, and certainly does not want to be in the position of questioning or second-guessing a superior's judgment too often.

In his research, Benson (1985, 589) found similar rational-izations, and claimed that many white-collar offenders employ these techniques to deny their "guilt and inner anguish" and to "avoid stigmatization as a criminal" (p. 605). Sutherland (1945) made several similar observations about corporate criminals. First, though they have violated the law, corporate criminals do not perceive of themselves as criminals, rationalizing that they are good, upstanding citizens. Second, corporate offenders protect their identity because they do not lose status among their peers, using peer evaluations to override and neutralize society's or the law's negative judgments. And third, corporate criminals express contempt for laws restricting their behaviors (they condemn the condemners). Consequently, factors that might normally deter a person from committing a corporate crime are effectively eliminated through the social-psychologi-cal process of neutralization.

The Social Psychology of Organizations

The importance of organizational behavior in contributing to corporate crimes should already be evident. Organizations, by their very nature, create a climate in which personal responsibility is *reduced* and the individual is *absorbed* into a larger whole which the individual may feel unable to control. This generates communication difficulties and makes it very easy for the left hand not to know what the right hand is doing. Frequently, corporate crimes occur out of ignorance—no single individual possesses all of the information necessary to appreciate possible dangers.

In other instances, organizations serve to depress individual initiative, which limits the extent to which employees will act as internal "police." Because organizational roles are clearly defined, health and safety concerns which fall outside of the individual's official sphere of authority are neglected.

Interpersonal relationships within organizations may also keep individuals from alerting superiors to these crimes. Although a person may know that a decision made by an associate is likely to cause harm or create the risk of harm, loyalty to a friend and unwillingness to make the friend look bad to superiors may serve to keep employees from speaking up about these problems. Moreover, as Jackall (1988) observes, corporate norms reinforce the more or less normal tendency to protect one's friends. "One has an obligation of sorts to cover up the real or presumed mistakes of one's immediate associates, at least by keeping quiet" (p. 128).

The roles of upper and middle management in the creation and toleration of corporate crime is also important. Upper management is responsible for establishing goals, creating a climate within which the production and design of dangerous products are either deplored or tolerated, and for establishing a style of communication which either fosters or inhibits the transmission of "bad news" (Clinard 1983, 71-74). Some top managers show a consistent concern with unsafe production techniques, or unsafe working conditions. This concern creates a climate in which lower level employees feel free to communicate their concerns to upper management. Even here, however, subordinates might believe that superiors are displeased when unsafe conditions are exposed. Thus, subordinates may participate in efforts to keep superiors from finding out about unsafe practices in order to avoid reprimands or other sanctions.

Other managers send messages which clearly indicate that meeting a production or product development goal is more important than anything else. In some corporations, upper management deliberately insulates itself from "bad news" so that top-level managers will not have to take responsibility should problems arise. "[H]igher ups do not inquire about what is going on and the lower levels do not tell them" (Clinard and Yeager 1980, 45). Organizations also create their own cultures with values which are either conducive or inhibitory of crimes (e.g., see, Nalla and Newman 1990, 122-138). For example, the corporate environment may establish conditions in which the transmission or learning of deviant values occurs freely (Sutherland 1949). The implication here is that the opportunity to encounter deviant norms, expectations and techniques varies from one organization to the next (Sutherland 1949). This view incorporates both structural (organizational) and individual (learning and the willingness to adopt deviant values) factors that may explain corporate crime.

We turn now to a review of explicitly macro-level explanations of corporate crime. Criminologists have tended to prefer macro-level to micro-level explanations when discussing corporate crime, arguing that "business crime is so pervasive, it can hardly be accidental to our system. Thus, we must seek the conditions of our society out of which corporate crime emerges as common practice" (Balkan *et al.* 1980, 174).

CORPORATE CRIME: MACRO-LEVEL EXPLANATIONS

Macro-level corporate crime research generally makes one of two different claims. The first implies that corporate crime is a direct result of the immediate organizational context in which social actors are located (e.g., Clinard and Yeager 1980; Coleman 1985, 220-227; Sutherland 1949). This research tries to pinpoint the organizational pressures and structures most conducive to crime. The second variety of macro-explanation examines wider or broader structural variables such as class structure or economic system variables thought to contribute to corporate crime. In this view, organizational structures, organizational behavior and the behavior of individuals are seen as affected and constrained by a larger set of structural variables. Thus, the tendency is to suggest how broad political-economic forces affect the type and amount of corporate crime found in a society and within organizations. We believe that both types of analyses are important, and that there is a definite need to consider the more immediate, organizational as well as the broader, political-economic context in which corporate crime is created (Groves and Lynch 1990). We will have more to say about this later. For now, let us review a few of the many structural explanations of corporate crime.

Anomie and Corporate Crime

Some corporate crime researchers employ well-known theories originally designed to explain ordinary or street crime in their discussions of the causes of corporate crime. For example, Merton's (1938) theory of anomie, which explains crime in terms of strains and pressures that result from a disjunction between culturally prescribed goals and structurally available means, has been used on several occasions as an explanation of corporate crime (e.g., see Passas 1990; Box 1983, 34-36; Vaughn 1982). Merton argued that everyone in American society is socialized to accept the same goal. However, not everyone has access to the legitimate means necessary to achieve material success goals. People whose success aspirations are blocked in this way experience strain, alienation and normlessness or anomie. They might respond to this situation by inventing or "innovating" illegal ways of obtaining material success.

In the corporate crime literature, Passas claims that a similar situation occurs within corporations, and argues that both organizational and structural goals create pressures to achieve. If available legitimate means fail to help the corporation meet established goals, or if legitimate means for achieving goals are inefficient or unavailable, corporate criminals invent new means to achieve culturally and organizationally selected goals. Thus, when legitimate means are blocked, those experiencing the strain associated with a failure to fulfill culturally or organizationally inspired aspirations may create illegal ways of successfully fulfilling both organizational and structural goals (Passas 1990, 161-162; see also Groves and Sampson 1987). This view describes both the immediate and broader structural conditions that motivate and/or provide individuals with the opportunity to commit corporate crime.

Environmental Uncertainty

An "environmental uncertainty approach" has also been advanced as a means of explaining the structural strains that might generate corporate crime. In some respects, this approach is similar to the anomie argument reviewed above. In this view, the sources of strain (environmental uncertainty) include excessive competition within an industry, a competitor's control of a new form of technology that makes production faster and cheaper, governmental regulations that drive up the cost of production, and increased labor union demands. As Box (1983,37) argues, "[w]hen ...environmental uncertainties increase,...the strain toward corporate criminal activity will increase." When corporate executives feel that environmental uncertainties are largely out of their control, the conditions conducive to crimes like espionage, arson, and the design and manufacturing of faulty products are in place (for extended discussion of other environmental uncertainties, see Box 1983, 35-37; Barnett 1981; Finney and Lesieur 1982, 269-275).

The Economic Structure and Corporate Crime

A very broad structural approach to corporate crime is found in the work of a number of radical criminologists who examine the connection between economic structures and corporate crime (e.g., Messerschmidt 1986, 99-129; Michalowski 1985, 314-359; Reiman 1990; Michalowski and Kramer 1987; Balkan *et al.* 1980, 164-185; Gordon 1971, 59; Chambliss 1975, 1984; Pearce 1976). In the radical view, the location of powerful individuals in the class and corporate structure is seen as providing them with the opportunity and motivation to commit corporate crime and to violate laws specifically designed to deter corporate offenses (Gordon 1971; Chambliss 1975, 167; Balkan et al., 1980,175). In addition, these powerful people can also influence the scope of law, and how or whether law is applied to corporations (Chambliss and Seidman 1982). More specifically, radical criminologists suggest ways in which the economic and ideological structure of corporate capitalism creates an environment in which anything goes, as long as the outcome furthers the goal of capital accumulation. This argument, which is similar to Merton's strain argument in many ways (Groves and Sampson 1987) suggests that the ideological environment of corporate capitalism places great stress on profit making, and creates a consumer culture and a corporate culture designed to stimulate and feed the needs of consumers (e.g., Henry 1963). Both cultures revolve around and exaggerate production and consumption patterns (Veblen 1899). As Balkan *et al.* (1980, 164) note, "corporate crime supports and satisfies accumulation...." Let us take a closer look at this explanation.

A basic tenet of radical analysis is that capitalism is based upon accumulation. As Marx (1977, chapter 24, section 3) noted, profit is the "Moses and the Prophet" of capitalism. By this, Marx meant that profit is the ultimate driving force behind capitalism. Consequently, profit or accumulation is the ultimate good or justification for behavior in a capitalist system. This goal is the very basis upon which corporations are founded.

Profit, created by extracting surplus value or unpaid labor from the production process, can be increased in two ways: by reducing costs or by increasing sales (see Lynch and Groves 1989, 10, 63-64,123-124 for further discussion). Costs can be reduced if the amount of human labor used to produce a quantity of goods can be decreased. To do so, corporations replace human labor with machine labor (or replace high-priced labor with cheaper labor). And, so long as the price of the goods and the amount of goods sold remains the same (or increases), profit increases. By replacing human labor with machine labor, corporations can even increase their profits where consumption of their product has fallen. Replacing human labor with machine labor, however, has severe negative consequences for society as a whole, since it generates a marginal population of unemployed and underemployed workers. Businesses typically viewed this as the "cost of doing business" and as a natural but regrettable outcome. Radicals, on the other hand, suggest that the cost-benefit concerns which motivate companies to replace human labor with machine labor for the sake of profit could themselves be viewed as crimes that violate human rights (Schwendinger and Schwendinger 1970; see also: Balkan *et al.* 1980, 52-56; Quinney 1980; Marx 1977).

The second way to elevate profit is to increase consumer consumption of goods. The logic here is simple: If the amount (and price) of labor used in production and the price of the commodity remain the same, but the quantity of goods sold can be increased, then the corporation's profit increases.

In short, to profit, the corporate sector must either ensure that consumption is continually increased, or that labor costs are continually suppressed (Marx 1974). In pursuing both these tactics for the sake of profit alone—a characteristic of the corporations that is greatly exaggerated under conditions of monopoly capitalism evident in the US (Baran and Sweezy 1966)—corporations often violate laws. For example, companies might market inferior goods because making the products safer would require more labor or more costly raw materials or more planning and a better design. Corporations might even expose their workers to unsafe working environments and working conditions, since making the workplace safe is a capital expense that eats up profits. Or, corporations might choose not to install costly safety equipment to protect the environment from industrial pollution. Or, corporations might artificially create demand for a product through advertising. While advertising itself is not illegal, false advertising is, and many companies claim that their product is better or safer, even when it is the same as the product offered by competitors. In recent years, there has been growing concern over unethical advertising, such as targeting cigarette advertising to the young and minorities or targeting minority communities for high alcohol beer and wine. While not currently illegal, these latter activities are certainly questionable, and it could be argued that targeting specific groups to stimulate the consumption of products known to be hazardous should be illegal.

Thus, as Michalowski (1985, 325-330) argues, the profit maximization motive in a capitalist system leads to maximum prices, attempts to maximize sales, and attempts to minimize the cost of labor and raw materials used in production. It also leads to a minimal attempt to protect non-corporate actors from corporate crime (Balkan *et al.* 1980: Quinney 1980). In minimizing costs and maximizing sales, corporations often violate consumer health and safety laws, regulatory laws regarding safe workplace production techniques, environmental protection and pollution laws, advertising laws, etc., that place workers, consumers and the general public at an increased risk of injury, illness and death (Michalowski 1985, 331-344; Reiman 1990, 57-78; see also Messerschmidt 1986).

MACRO AND MICRO CONCERNS IN CONTEXT

Above, we reviewed a variety of explanations for corporate crime. We began with a few of the many micro or individual theories used to explain the occurrence of corporate crime, and moved to an examination of two different types of macro-theory: those that take the organizational structure as a starting point, and those that begin with society as the unit of analysis. Each view has certain advantages and disadvantages. For example, the advantage of micro theories is that they give us specific information about individuals and the reasons that they commit crime. Micro theories cannot, however, tell us about crime trends, such as why the crime rate goes up or down. Another criticism of micro theories is that even though they are about individuals, they are a very poor means of accurately predicting exactly who will commit crime. An advantage of organizational theories is that they are a bit more accurate (statistically) to the extent that they provide a better gauge of upward and downward trends in corporate crime. However, organizational macro-theories tell us little about the types of individuals within a corporation who become involved in corporate crime. Structural level macro-theories, because they begin with social structure, culture or economic and political system variables, can be criticized for giving us very little information about individuals. In short, structural theories are the farthest removed from the individual. On the positive side, structural theories appear to be the most accurate when it comes to predicting crime trends.

Recognizing that each type of theory answers only a fraction of the question, "what causes crime?" criminologists have increasingly argued for a perspective that integrates micro and macro level theory (Messner *et al.* 1989; Katz 1988). In short, criminologists have increasingly recognized that each type of theory provides information about different aspects of crime. As far as corporate crime is concerned, micro-theories tell us about the individuals who commit these crimes; organizational theories tell us about the types of organizational structures most likely to generate corporate crime; structural theories tell us about the types of societies, cultures, political and economic systems in which we are most likely to find corporate crimes of violence. The problem is, "how do we go about integrating these different levels of analysis in order to create an effective explanation of corporate crime?"

The Need for Integrated Theory

The need for an integrated approach to social problems is not new. C. Wright Mills (1959) long ago argued for an integrated approach to understanding a variety of social problems. He called this way of thinking about social problems the "sociological imagination."

Mills believed that "The sociological imagination enables its possessor to understand the larger historical scene in terms of its meaning for the life and external career of a variety of individuals" (p.5). What Mills meant was that individuals who live in the same society, who share common experiences like class location, community, work environments and culture, are often subjected to and must react to a very similar set of pressures, constraints and stimuli (a milieu). Individuals do not construct their reactions to these milieux experiences out of nothing. People often react to situations they encounter based upon prior knowledge and a common culture. Because individuals are socialized into a common culture, they often react in a similar fashion to stimuli they encounter in life. These similar reactions make up the statistical trends social scientists often discover in their research. Consequently, if we can understand the societal, economic and organizational structures in which people are enmeshed and socialized, we know something about the frame of reference within which people select from a more or less limited range of structured choices (Groves and Frank 1987). In Mills' words, "to understand the changes of many personal milieux we are required to look beyond them" (1958, 10) and to link biography (the individual) to history (social structure); or in short, to connect the micro and macro levels of analysis.

This is not an easy task, and the first hurdle we encounter concerns a starting point: Should we begin at the macro or the micro level? There is no solution to this problem, and the choice of a starting point reflects the theorist's own personal biases (Groves and Lynch 1990, 362-365). Even Marx and Engels (1970, 29), two well-known macro-level theorists, recognized the importance of both micro and macro variables. This idea is summarized in their famous saying: "Circumstances make men, just as much as men make circumstances." By this they implied that individuals may create the social environment, but once created the social environment exerts certain pressures on individuals and tends to make them behave in a similar fashion. Individuals can change the social environment, but they must do so within the social context that previous generations created. Thus, while individuals create their own behavior, they do so within the limits of an existing social structure that provides a predefined set of possible behaviors.

As structuralists, Marx and Engels preferred to begin at the macro level. This is where our preference lies as well. Below, we attempt to provide an integrated view of corporate crime. We limit our discussion to American culture and its economic system, capitalism.

An Integrated Theory of Corporate Crime

Capitalism is often defined as a profit-oriented system of production. But capitalism is much more: it is a *class* system of production where access to, or relationship to, the means used to create wealth defines the types of opportunities and life chances people can enjoy (e.g., Groves and Frank 1987). Simply put, this means that the higher an individual's social class, the more opportunities and chances for success the person can access. The reverse statement would apply to persons from the lowest social classes: the lower a person's social class, the less access they have to opportunities for success.

For our discussion of corporate crime, two classes are most important: (1) the class that owns the technology, machinery and factories that makes modern production possible—the capitalist class, and (2) the petty-bourgeoisie, the class that manages the capitalist's holdings, factories, banks, etc.,. We focus on these two classes because, as Sutherland noted, only those from a particular social location can commit corporate crime. How can these observations be employed to create an integrated theory that meets our previous definition of good theory?

First, we should entertain the idea that both organization's and individual's desires for success, wealth, money and prestige are influenced by the type of social system in which that individual or organization is located. If the social system overemphasizes certain desires, these desires may become an obsession, and the entire social system may be designed to achieve these valued items regardless of the costs involved. Thus, we need to be cognizant of the fact that individual desires and corporate goals are shaped by the larger environment in which they exist. In capitalist systems, this means that money will be an important goal and motivator.

Second, class location, and the effect class location has on crime should be addressed. Class location, as noted above, provides the opportunities to commit certain types of crime. In addition to providing the opportunity to commit a corporate crime, the class (structural) location of the capitalist and the petty bourgeoisie may also motivate them to commit corporate crimes of violence. As we noted above, the lure of profit is strong in a capitalist system. Consequently, even those at the top experience structurally induced pressures to succeed which translate into material and monetary desires (e.g., as previously noted, this is the basic idea behind the theory of Anomie). However, while all corporate officials are exposed to these strains and have similar opportunities to commit corporate crimes of violence, not all corporate officials are criminals. Why is it that structurally induced pressures to succeed affect some individuals but not others?

One answer is that the organizational context in which different corporate executives are located either facilitates or impedes criminal behavior. For example, some corporate officials may be socialized into a corporate or organizational structure in which violating the law is expected or considered normal (Sutherland). These officials might be more likely than those in other corporations to engage in crime. In other words, some corporate criminals learn to become corporate criminals because the corporation in which they work exaggerates the "natural" tendency of capitalist organizations and places extraordinary emphasis on values such as success, obedience, and expediency. These individuals, in short, find themselves in a corporate environment in which the pressure to succeed creates criminal responses.

Crime-prone corporations do not spring up out of thin air. The structure of a corporation, the values it emphasizes, and the means its devises to succeed in its chosen task are influenced by broader cultural, economic and political forces. These forces might include the type of economic system, the state of the economy (environmental uncertainties), and the degree to which law enforcement is sensitive to particular types of violations of law. In other words, all corporations are in the same boat. They all must respond to the economic structure of which they are a part. However, conditions may also vary for specific corporations, given the type of commodity they produce and sensitivity of law enforcement officials to violations of legal codes that affect particular industries.

Corporations that promote illegal behavior may do so because of the pressure on the corporation to turn a profit. Companies in highly competitive markets where profits are spread over a number of firms, and companies that have been "underachievers" or have had poor performance records seem to violate the law more often than other types of firms (Barnett 1981; Finney and Lesieur 1982). These corporations are more motivated to commit crime than other corporations because they feel the capitalist pressures of the market more fiercely. Thus, the pressures to succeed experienced by all corporate officials may be intensified for a segment of corporate leaders who work in "crime prone" corporate organizations. There is little doubt that such organizations exist. For example, Sutherland's (1949, 1983) examination of adverse legal decisions against 70 of America's largest corporations revealed that 98 percent were recidivists, and that the average number of decisions against each corporation was fourteen.

A second answer to why some individuals engage in crime while others do not may be found within micro theories. This is an important factor to consider, because not all corporate officials, even if they work in the same crime-prone corporation, engage in illegal behavior. As reviewed above, some criminologists argue that people have different characteristics that may make them more likely to commit criminal acts. People who are ruthless or daring, for instance, may be more likely to take risks and violate the law. If we place this person in an organizational structure in which violating the law is viewed as normal corporate behavior, the probability that a crime will occur is increased.

In short, some corporate actors succumb to pressures in the corporate environment while others do not. Since there is little research which examines the personality characteristics of corporate offenders, anything we may say in this respect is conjecture. However, the research that does exist suggests that persons who commit corporate crimes are not exactly like everyone else. As Box, Reckless, Hirschi and Gottfredson and Jeffrey implied (see above), these people appear reckless or cunning and willing to take chances, calculating that the chance that they get caught is minimal. Given these few characteristics, what we can say is that there appears to be a connection or correlation between the characteristics of corporate criminals and the characteristics of people who work in corporations. In other words, to be successful within the context of corporate capitalism, a person is required to be cunning and to calculate the costs and rewards of acting in a particular way. Such people are not only attracted to corporate jobs, but are sought out by corporations (Box 1983). Jackall (1988) has observed that individuals who repeatedly "buck the system" by asking moral questions that make their colleagues and superiors "uncomfortable" are not likely to be promoted. If they persist, they will eventually be "let go."

One final point that is needed in a good theory is the element of law enforcement or social control. This factor impacts corporations and corporate executives in a number of different ways. First, both corporations and individuals make an assessment of how big a risk they undertake if they choose to commit crimes. If there is little enforcement of the laws that pertain to the corporation, or if the enforcement agencies assigned to detect violations of law are small and underfunded, corporate actors might decide that the rewards from committing crime are greater than the chance of being apprehended. But, remember—those occupying positions within this corporation must first be motivated to commit a crime.

Second, as we noted earlier in this book, social structure influences the amount and type of law that is applied to corporate criminals. In discussing conflict theories, we noted that some theorists conclude that corporations and corporate executives are able to use their power to ensure that little law is applied to corporate crime. Further, when the law is applied, corporations generally face small, civil fines when they violate the law. Well-funded corporations may lobby to have the constraints of law eased or derail attempts to institute new laws.

Briefly, our integrated theory of corporate crime suggests that the following factors should be addressed: (1) how the economic structure establishes conditions conducive to violent crimes that generate profits; (2) how class membership affects the opportunity and motivation to engage in corporate crime; (3) how opportunity and motivation may be affected by the specific corporate context in which an individual is located; (4) how corporations may be organized to employ illegal and dangerous means to generate profit; (5) how deviance prone corporations may establish conditions which foster the learning of criminal techniques, motives and rationalizations; and (6) how personality characteristics may intersect with corporate goals and values to create crime.

Our "theory," as stated here, is not complete. It provides only the skeleton for thinking about corporate crime in a contextual and integrated fashion. We offer this discussion, not as a definitive explanation of corporate crime, but merely as a means of suggesting the ways in which different levels of theory may be used to explain corporate crime.

Conclusion

This chapter examined a variety of ways of thinking about the causes of corporate crime. There are no answers at this point in time to the question "what causes corporate crime." There are simply answers that more or less fit the criteria for a good theory of crime that we offered earlier in this chapter. It is up to each of you to decide which theories meet these criteria.

We would like to mention one more point before moving on. That point involves the *types* of explanations theorists use to explain corporate crime. Notice that many of the theories do not suggest factors like poverty, poor family upbringing and background, ecological factors, or a whole slew of other factors used to explain crimes of the lower class. This may be because corporate crimes are caused by a different set of factors; or it may be that a general theory of crime is incapable of explaining both the crimes of the powerful and powerless simultaneously. More than likely, the lack of overlap here occurs because corporate crime has not been a major concern of criminologists. In addition, it may be that the explanation for corporate crimes, even those which entail violence, is too obvious—profit. Thus, we do not feel the need to develop elaborate explanations of corporate crime because it is obviously motivated by greed. But, we could say as much for ordinary crimes, since 90 percent or more of those crimes are also committed for monetary reasons. In short, maybe our lack of interest in corporate crime is related to our fascination with the unusual. Corporate crimes, as discussed earlier, are not unusual. They are extremely widespread in our society. Street crimes, however, particularly those that involve violence, are, statistically speaking, much more unusual than corporate violence (Reiman 1990).

Eight

Controlling Corporate Violence

STUDENTS OF the criminal justice system are familiar with the functions of the police, the courts, and the correctional system in fighting conventional crimes of violence. Corporate violence involves a different set of actors, however. Examples like those in Chapter 4, in which the Ford Motor Company and Film Recovery Systems were prosecuted for homicide, are extremely rare. In most cases, control of these crimes is routinized in a system of regulatory enforcement, carried out by a diverse set of agencies having widely differing powers and patterns of operation (see Chapter 5, Table 5.1).

Given the broad variation in the ways in which these agencies operate, it is difficult to draw any hard and fast generalizations about regulatory enforcement and the control of corporate violence. In this chapter we will review:

1. The three primary legal mechanisms invoked against these crimes and some of the general issues involved in preventing and discovering these crimes.

2. The relative advantages and disadvantages of these mechanisms.

3. Some of the barriers to effective prevention of corporate violence.

OVERLAPPING SYSTEMS OF CONTROL

Several independent systems of law are available and may be used simultaneously to combat crimes of corporate violence. When individuals are injured, they may bring private civil suits against the persons or corporations responsible for the injury. The government may also step in, either through instituting a criminal action against an offending person or corporation or by using a variety of administrative, regulatory mechanisms to force offenders to correct violations. To bring a civil action, a victim must actually suffer an injury. Criminal and administrative action may be used even if no one has actually been injured. These regulations can be used when there is a potential for injury. The act of creating the risk of harm is often sufficient to trigger criminal or administrative remedies.

Private Civil Suits

Private civil suits have become an important means of controlling corporations. In recent years, large corporations have been forced to pay multimillion dollar damage awards to victims. Frequently, civil damages awarded in private suits are many times greater than the maximum fine that the government could impose in a criminal or civil action. An additional advantage of civil suits over criminal prosecution or regulatory action is that the victims are compensated for the injuries they have suffered. Rather than a fine simply being paid into government coffers, those who have been injured are compensated, however inadequately, for the illness, pain, and suffering they have endured. When private civil suits are employed, individuals who suffer injuries or deprivations become the people responsible for "policing" corporate misbehavior.

Unfortunately, experts disagree concerning the effectiveness of private civil suits as a general deterrent to prevent corporate crime. Some believe that the fear of a large civil award against a company and the bad publicity that accompanies court action are strong deterrents which keep companies from taking unreasonable risks. Being forced to pay a large damage award would lower profits and make the company less attractive to investors, thereby decreasing the firm's capacity to prosper and expand. Since corporate managers have a personal stake in the health and vitality of the corporation, they should avoid taking risks that might lead to successful civil suits against the corporation.

Others disagree, however, pointing to examples in which corporate managers have made explicit decisions to risk getting sued because the costs of paying settlements to victims would be less than the cost of making corrections to prevent the injury in the first place. This was allegedly the situation that led the Ford Motor Company to decide not to fix the gas tank design on the Ford Pinto in the 1970s (see Chapter 4). Civil suits are often less costly than correcting health and safety hazards, which might require redesigning a product or retooling a factory. Private suits are not the most feasible response for all individuals because of the costs involved in hiring a private attorney to file a law suit against the company responsible for causing illness and injury.

Oftentimes, the victims of corporate violence are not aware that they are victims. A person is diagnosed as having cancer, but is unaware that the cancer was caused by toxic chemicals that were dumped into a lake. Even if the cause of the disease or injury is known or suspected, identifying the responsible person or corporation can still be difficult. This was initially one of the problems asbestosis victims had in suing for damages. Victims usually could not identify precisely which asbestos manufacturer produced the asbestos to which they were exposed. Until the courts consolidated the asbestos cases in a class action, victims were unable to successfully sue any of the manufacturers.

Even if a specific cause is identified and the responsible party is known, other problems still impede a successful suit against those responsible. In many cases, the amount of harm suffered by any single individual is too small to warrant the expense of litigation. Only those victims that have been seriously injured and who are, therefore, suing for large damage awards, will be able to afford the legal expenses of bringing this type of suit. In addition, civil suits require extensive investigation. Technical experts are often needed to testify to the hazards alleged by the victim. These factors increase the costs of litigation and further decrease the pool of victims who can afford to sue for damages.

Because of the costs involved in bringing these suits, the number of suits actually filed is often only a small fraction of the total number of victims. Consequently, when analyzing their likelihood of being sued, corporations need not worry about compensating *all* victims, but only those with sufficient resources to successfully sue the corporation. The costs of defending against these suits and paying damages are often less than the costs of correcting the hazard. Thus, the threat of civil suits may not be an adequate deterrent.

Criminal Prosecution

Typically, criminal prosecution is used as a last resort, when all other efforts to gain compliance have failed or in response to a particularly outrageous violation. One reason for not using criminal penalties is the relative difficulty of using the criminal system rather than the more streamlined administrative system. Because of the rights to which defendants are entitled in criminal court, the heavier burden of proof on the government in a criminal prosecution, and the technical complexity of these cases, criminal cases are hard to win. In addition, the meager penalties frequently imposed by courts following criminal conviction discourage prosecutors from using criminal prosecution more frequently.

The difficulties of prosecution aside, opinions differ regarding the appropriateness of criminal punishment, particularly imprisonment, for crimes involving corporate violence (Fisse 1986, 24). As indicated in Chapter Four, public opinion favors using criminal penalties and jail sentences in appropriate cases of corporate violence. Despite examples in this book of severe penalties and even jail sentences, in most cases criminal penalties are extremely lenient. Judges have shown a good deal of unwillingness to impose serious criminal penalties (Reiman 1990). Offenders receive the lenient treatment usually afforded first-time offenders. Judges frequently consider it inappropriate to send middle-class offenders to jail with "common criminals" (Clinard and Yeager 1980, 289). Because of the higher status of corporate managers who are responsible for acts of corporate violence, the trauma of prosecution itself is frequently viewed as sufficient punishment. Similarly, if the defendant has suffered negative publicity as a result of prosecution, judges are likely to consider bad publicity as "punishment enough." Finally, since defendants frequently are able to play a shell game with the question of responsibility, they argue that the violation was accidental and that the court has no reason to suspect that similar violations would occur in the future.

Punishment is further complicated when the defendant is a corporation rather than an individual. Because of the difficulties of proving personal responsibility, prosecution frequently proceeds only against the corporation (Yoder 1978). In these instances, the only sanctions that are typically available are fines, which some commentators fear are looked upon by offending corporations as merely a "cost of doing business" (Fisse 1986, 26, 27-29). Because corporations cannot be put in jail, some scholars have suggested that the justice system needs to design creative alternatives for sanctioning corporations that break the law (Coffee 1981) .

Braithwaite (1985, 166-167) summarizes a number of creative solutions to the problem of punishing corporations:

Equity Fines. The company is ordered to issue new shares

[of stock] to a victim compensation fund. After a 5 percent equity fine, the victim compensation fund will own 5 percent of the share in the company, and the remaining shareholders will have the value of their holding diluted by 5 percent (Coffee 1981; Fisse and Braithwaite 1984).

Publicity Orders. The court orders placement of advertisements or other publicity in mass media outlets notifying or warning the public (or certain publics) of a company's offense (Fisse and Braithwaite 1983).

Internal Discipline Orders. The company is ordered to investigate an offense committed on its behalf, to discipline culpable employees, and to report to the court on what it has found and done (Criminal Law and Penal Methods Reform Committee 1977, 361).

Preventive Orders. The company is ordered the change certain policies or standard operating procedures, expand certain internal compliance activities or budgets, appoint persons to new positions with specified authority to prevent future offending (Solomon and Nowak 1980; Criminal Law and Penal Methods Reform Committee 1977, 359; Stone 1975, 186-98).

Corporate Probation. A relevant expert is appointed under a corporate probation order to supervise implementation of internal reforms similar to those under preventive orders (Yoder 1978, p. 53; Yale Law Journal 1979).

Community Service Orders. The company is ordered to perform as an organization some work of community service relevant to its expertise (e.g., a coal miner testing a new approach to revegetating reclaimed strip-mining land) (Fisse 1981).

Regulatory Justice

Because of the difficulties posed by private civil suits and criminal prosecution, the most common response to corporate violence occurs through the regulatory system. Through specialization and the application of specialized investigatory and enforcement tools, the regulatory system holds special advantages in controlling corporate violence. The major drawback to regulatory justice is that it does not carry with it the stigma of criminal conviction. Consequently, corporate violence is treated differently—probably more leniently—than conventional violent crimes.

History of the Regulatory System

Regulation of health and safety began in earnest toward the end of the nineteenth century, when the negative effects of industrialization were beginning to be felt by an increasing number of consumers, workers, and the general public. Initially, regulation was carried out primarily by individual states, and regulatory action during the late nineteenth century through the middle of the twentieth century served to curtail some of the more dangerous practices (Meier 1985). It also laid the foundation for expanding corporate responsibility for the protection of health and safety.

During the 1970s, the regulatory system grew at an enormous pace. Some of the largest and most powerful federal agencies were created during this decade. Each of these agencies was given a mandate related to the protection of the public from certain risks, whether exposure to toxic chemicals or the ingestion of carcinogenic additives or the risk of falling from an unguarded catwalk.

A variety of powers was given to these agencies, including the power to conduct regular inspections of factories, to require the review of products prior to offering them for sale, the power to deny or revoke licenses, the authority to impose civil fines, and the opportunity to seek criminal charges. Although criminal penalties are commonly viewed as the most serious sanction that can be brought against a violator, probably due to the stigma that attaches upon criminal conviction, regulatory sanctions often carry a more potent penalty. Revocation of a license, for example, can put a company out of business by forbidding it to engage in its normal business activities.

The rapid growth of regulation during the 1970s amounted to a revolution in the breadth and effectiveness of regulation. The creation of new regulations created friction with the regulated industries, which chafed at having a government agency prying into what previously had been private management decisions. In many instances, the expansion of the powers and responsibilities of regulatory agencies during the 1970s resulted in a backlash during the 1980s. Corporations fought hard to slash agency budgets, prevent vigorous enforcement, and reduce the number and stringency of regulations. For these and other reasons, regulators frequently must surmount obstacles in the investigation and enforcement of corporate violence.

Special Problems in Fighting Corporate Violence

Fighting corporate violence involves four related types of activities: (1) investigations to discover violations, (2) investigation to build a case against the violator, (3) efforts to obtain compliance voluntarily, and (4) initiation of formal legal action to halt the violation or sanction the violator. Although enforcement officials have a wide array of enforcement tools at their disposal for investigating these crimes, more tools in fact than are available to police for the investigation of conventional crimes, enforcement officials frequently find it difficult to be successful in their efforts.

One of the difficulties in enforcing the laws relating to health and safety is the role of the victim of these crimes. As noted above in the context of private civil suits, victims are rarely a source of information about these crimes because they are generally unaware that they have been victimized. For example, the driver who experiences a tire blow-out on the highway and is injured in the resulting accident is unaware that the blow-out was not the result of normal "bad luck" but rather caused by a defect in the manufacture of the tire. The parents of a deformed child are more likely to blame themselves than to blame a drug company which may have marketed a drug without adequately testing the drug for its effects on the development of fetuses.

Even if the victim suspects that his/her problems are the result of a crime against health and safety, there is little that the victim is able to do. The former chemical plant worker who is dying of cancer may suspect that some chemical in the work environment caused the cancer, but lacking any knowledge of what chemical it might be, much less any evidence that a particular chemical caused this particular cancer, the illness is not reported to enforcement authorities. Because of the limited role victims play in the discovery of corporate violence (in stark contrast to the victim role in traditional crimes such as assault or rape), enforcement agencies need to rely upon alternative means of obtaining information about violations. Consequently, the investigation of crimes of corporate violence depends heavily on routine inspection and information provided to the enforcement agency by regulated firms.

Special Tools for Investigating Corporate Violence

Before police officers investigating a conventional crime may enter a home or business to look for evidence of the crime, the officers must have probable cause and, except in special circumstances, must have a search warrant. Regulatory investigators, in contrast, have been given authority to enter and inspect private establishments without warrants and without probable cause.

For example, food inspectors enter and inspect establishments engaged in food processing or storage. Worker safety and health inspectors investigate the conditions within factories and other work places, searching for violations of regulatory requirements. If violations are discovered in the course of these inspections, evidence may be collected which is admissible in either a criminal or a civil action against the firm or against particular individuals. (For more information on this topic, see Frank, 1986).

Another special tool allows regulatory investigators to collect information from potential violators regarding their conduct. Regulatory agencies require regulated firms to submit various kinds of information about their activities and products. For example, drug manufacturers must submit drug test data, automobile manufacturers must submit data regarding the functioning of safety features, chemical plants must submit records indicating the types of pollutants produced at their plants, and dairy plants must submit detailed records of bacteriological tests on milk received by the plant.

Criminal prosecution or civil penalties may rest entirely on information required under these provisions. Additional charges may be brought if the corporation provides false information to the regulatory agency. Critics of these procedures argue that they require firms and individuals to incriminate themselves, violating their Fifth Amendment rights. Without such provisions, however, many health and safety regulations would be virtually unenforceable.

Barriers to Effective Enforcement

In spite of these extraordinary enforcement powers, investigating and prosecuting corporate violence remains a very difficult task, frequently resulting in a great deal of effort with little to show for it in the end. The enforcement of health and safety law must overcome a number of barriers if it is to be effective.

Scholars differ in their assessments of the most significant barriers to regulatory effectiveness. Pluralist theorists tend to focus on organizational factors, such as insufficient resources, limited expertise, insufficient incentives to take formal action, and an organizational philosophy of voluntary compliance. Conflict theorists, on the other hand, focus their criticisms of the regulatory system on corporate sector influence over regulatory policy which effectively restrains the zeal of enforcement officials.

Insufficient Resources. Most government bureaucracies complain that their resources are inadequate to their tasks. In the case of regulatory enforcement agencies, this complaint is especially valid. Although one of the primary investigatory tools is the routine inspection, few enforcement agencies have sufficient personnel to conduct inspections more frequently than once every year. In many cases, only a fraction of the regulated establishments are inspected even that often (e.g., see Calivita 1983). As a result, violations may persist undiscovered for several years.

Similar problems plague those enforcement programs that depend upon the analysis of information submitted by regulated firms. The quantity of information submitted frequently overwhelms the ability of staff to collate and analyze it. Consequently, rather than doing their own independent analysis of the data, the enforcement agency frequently accepts the assertions of the regulated firm that all is well.

This situation is not only ineffective, it also creates some counter-productive side-effects. Regulated firms resent having to submit data that is never really put to use. While the regulated firms are subject to penalties for submitting information late or failing to provide some information, the enforcement agency is under no constraints to do anything with the data that is submitted. As a result, corporations complain, not without some merit, about excessive regulatory paperwork.

Limited Expertise. Because these violations of the law involve technologically complex problems on the edge of scientific knowledge, it is often difficult for enforcement agencies to ascertain how serious a particular violation is. This uncertainty is further aggravated by inadequate training of enforcement personnel. Poorly trained inspectors overlook significant dangers that are present. In addition, if inspectors recognize their limited expertise, their confidence is eroded, making inspectors timid in confronting violators. Inspectors are reluctant to demand compliance when they are unsure about the real significance of the violation in relation to health and safety.

Lack of expertise also undermines the inspectors' credibility, making the regulated industry less respectful. In some cases, poor training also causes inspectors to focus their efforts on relatively trivial violations, annoying the regulated firms and doing little constructive good for protecting the public. This was a frequent complaint during the 1970s in relation to the federal Occupational Safety and Health Administration. While significant hazards were being ignored, poorly trained inspectors were enforcing trivial violations, such as cracked toilet seats in employee bathrooms.

Lack of Incentives to Take Formal Action. When regulatory officials discover violations that create a risk of injury or illness to consumers, workers, or the public, they have two main options for reacting to the discovery. They can institute formal enforcement action against the corporation or they can attempt to persuade the corporation to correct the violation voluntarily. Instituting formal action almost always requires more regulatory effort and expense than simply waiting for the violating firm to correct the violation voluntarily. Since most violators do eventually make corrections voluntarily and since formal action is difficult, expensive, and entails a large chance of failure, enforcement officials have little incentive to move forward with formal action.

In addition, because formal action is relatively rare, regulatory officials are often unfamiliar with the procedures required to bring an action and are especially worried about the prospect of making procedural errors which will cause the case to be thrown out. They may even worry about being embarrassed if they lose the case in court. Their legitimacy and authority might be undermined by confronting corporate violations, and then losing the battle. For this combination of reasons, regulatory officials often prefer to seek correction of violations through persuasion rather than enforcement.

The fact that violations usually only create a risk of harm, and that enforcement officials are not confronted with bleeding victims, also serves to diminish their motivation to pursue enforcement against violators. Although enforcement officials understand that violations increase the probability that someone will be hurt or become ill, or even be killed, the reality of this fact is easily forgotten. The victims are invisible.

The Philosophy of Voluntary Compliance. One of the primary criticisms that has been aimed at regulatory enforcement is the excessive reliance on persuasion and voluntary compliance. As noted above, most regulatory agencies depend on the violating firms to correct violations without the agency having to initiate formal enforcement action. This does work in most cases in which violations are discovered. Many corporations are cooperative and correct violations that are discovered by regulatory officials. For the worst offenders, however, a strategy of voluntary compliance can be a license to continue flouting the law and risking people's health. The origins of voluntary compliance strategies are found both in the nature of the regulatory task and the characteristics of the regulatory environment.

Because most violators do correct violations when they are pointed out by inspectors, an expectation is created in which all violators are treated as though they are cooperative. Consequently, enforcement officials respond by using persuasion, rather than legal action, to get violators to comply with the law. The expectation of cooperation is wrong, however, in those cases in which the corporation is unwilling to correct the violation voluntarily. When this error occurs in conjunction with a serious violation, very serious consequences can result.

Recall the situation involving Life Sciences Products (LSP) and Allied Chemical Corporation in the Kepone incident (see Chapter Four). In that case (Stone 1982, 290):

> The state Water Quality Control Board realized there was a serious problem of noncompliance during a routine check in October 1974 [almost a year before the Kepone plant was shut down by the state epidemiologist], when it discovered a huge pit filling with Kepone. At that time company and local sewage officials were to deal with the Kepone problem. The board had the authority to close the plant down (one of its people seems to have been so inclined), but decided to try persuasion instead...
>
> In autumn 1974, OSHA received a complaint from an LSP employee who claimed to have been fired for refusal to work under unsafe conditions. OSHA's response was merely to write LSP a letter of inquiry, to which LSP responded soothingly. OSHA accepted LSP's assurances without making any on-site investigation.

A misplaced reliance on voluntary compliance is also implicated in the death of Stefan Golab at the Film Recovery plant,
described in Chapter 4. Recall that OSHA inspectors had been
to the corporate offices and inspected the company's records
on safety and health in the plant. When the records indicated
that there were no problems in the plant, the inspector did not
bother to inspect the plant itself and observe the conditions
actually endured by employees in the plant.

In these and countless other examples, enforcement agencies can be observed relying on persuasion and deferring to
information provided by the corporation itself rather than
doing an independent inquiry. Why would an enforcement
agency patiently rely on persuasion and inspection of the
company's own records? Some of the reasons have been
discussed above. Conflict theorists, however, point to some
additional reasons, including agency capture and power politics.

Agency Capture. In at least some instances, excessive reliance on a voluntary compliance strategy appears to be related
to industry influence on regulatory policy. Many scholars of
regulatory enforcement have noted the tendency of regulatory
agencies to become captives of the industries they regulate
(Simon and Eitzen 1990, 17-21; Chambliss and Seidman 1982).
Regulatory capture is a process whereby the agency adopts the
values and orientation of the regulated industry. This frequently means that the agency adopts the same sorts of
neutralizations that firms do in discounting the seriousness of
violations.

For example, following the passage of the Motor Vehicle
Safety Act, the auto industry embarked on a lobbying campaign
designed to capture regulators in the Department of Transportation (Dowie 1977, 24). After the passage of the act, industry
lobbyists descended on the Department of Transportation to
begin the "education" of the auto safety bureaucrats.

> [The lobbyists'] job was to implant the industry ideology in
> the minds of the new officials regulating auto safety.
> Briefly summarized, that ideology states that auto safety

accidents are caused not by cars, but by 1) people and 2) highway conditions.

It is possible that such influences explain the weak fuel tank safety standards that were in effect at the time that the Pinto was designed and marketed.

There is no doubt that similar efforts are conducted in other regulatory agencies and that these efforts leave their mark (Simon and Eitzen 1990, 21-26). Julian Greenspan, former Deputy Chief of Litigation in the Justice Department, described the impact of agency capture in the Nuclear Regulatory Commission (*Corporate Crime Reporter* 1987b, 5-6):

> actions are taken to discourage field inspectors from reporting or aggressively following up on violations that they spot and reporting them to headquarters, or reporting them to the NRC's Office of Investigations which is supposed to do the misconduct type investigations. That is one thing, screening off or sheltering the ability of violations from coming to light. Then, in those instances where they do come to light or to the attention of people at the NRC that can investigate them, throwing monkey wrenches into those investigations by making gratuitous, exonerating statements concerning the subject's conduct, by tipping off subjects as to the direction and scope of investigation.

One reason that regulatory agency officials become advocates for the regulated firms rather than for the public that the regulations are designed to protect is that the public is distant and seldom heard. Because the public's perspective is usually not represented as frequently or as expertly, agency officials are faced with a one-sided perspective and one-sided information, in which the industry's arguments appear more and more reasonable. Agency officials begin to believe industry when it argues that it needs protection from excessive regulation or over-zealous enforcement agents.

This process of ideological conversion is the subtle side of regulatory politics. In some cases, a policy of voluntary compliance is the result of more overt political pressures. Since the regulatory agency is dependent upon the legislature or Congress for its resources, administrators of these agencies must be particularly careful not to make enemies in Congress or the legislature. Conversely, since violators frequently are politically active, with friends in "high places," they may be able to get a legislator to intervene to "call off" the agency watchdogs.

Legislators, in turn, may make veiled threats to cut the agency's budget or to hold investigatory hearings on the performance of the agency. While these threats are rarely carried out, regulatory officials are sensitive to their vulnerability. It becomes very difficult for enforcement officials to resist normative pressures to respond in a spirit of compromise. "Let's be reasonable" becomes the motto of many regulatory agencies. While reasonableness is an appropriate goal, too often "reasonableness" means placing the interests of the corporation ahead of the goal of protecting the public from the dangers of corporate violence.

Overzealous Enforcement

While criminologists and public interest groups have focused their attention primarily on the inadequacies of enforcement in relation to corporate violence, others—particularly economists and industry spokesmen—have complained of overzealous enforcement. One particular point of criticism was the "legalistic" approach undertaken by some federal agencies during the Carter administration. Rather than relying on voluntary compliance, regulatory officials made greater use of formal enforcement action and the use of penalties to deter violations.

Critics of the legalistic approach argue that it is both unfair and inefficient. Elaborate studies have been produced which purport to show that the expense of prosecution and abatement far exceed the benefits to the public.

Part of the controversy here stems from differing perspectives about the appropriate way in which the costs and benefits of regulation should be assessed. But the controversy also reflects a more fundamental difference in values. Although stringent enforcement strategies are usually discussed as a means of deterring corporate violence, in many cases the real motivation is retribution (for discussion see Braithwaite 1986). Proponents of strong measures typically view corporate violence in the same light as conventional crimes of violence. As such, these crimes merit the same harsh treatment afforded other violent crimes.

From this perspective, it matters little that the company voluntarily ceases the violation when ordered to do so by the enforcement agency. The issue of punishment remains: what consequences should befall a company that knowingly allowed a violation to continue until finally ordered to stop. This is precisely the issue raised by the judge in the Cordis pacemaker case when the he refused to go along with a lenient plea bargain worked out between prosecutors and corporate executives (see Chapter 4). Advocates of the legalistic approach clearly view these violations as deserving punishment, and assert that it is unfair and immoral to allow these acts of violence and recklessness to go unpunished.

Under the Reagan administration, legalistic enforcement was brought to a halt in federal agencies. "Voluntary compliance" became the official policy of the administration, emphasizing cooperation between industry and the government in attaining "substantial" compliance. The rationale for this policy was that legalistic enforcement is (1) unnecessary since most violators comply voluntarily, (2) unfair because most violations occur through oversight and are not culpable and therefore not deserving of punishment, and (3) counterproductive because legalistic enforcement creates friction and hostility between industry and the government, and makes even law-abiding firms less willing to comply unless they are forced to do so. Critics of the Reagan administration's program argued that this strategy was viewed by industry as a green light to ignore health and safety standards, reducing the fear of getting caught violating health and safety laws.

It is interesting to note, however, that while the Reagan Administration was criticized for introducing an overly conciliatory regulatory style, the use of criminal sanctions actually increased in some regulatory areas during the Reagan years. For example, environmental enforcement has included more frequent use of criminal prosecution during the 1980s. The reasons for this divergent pattern are not entirely clear. Some commentators have noted that the Reagan administration may have used criminal prosecution in particularly egregious cases to make an example of these offenders, to deter others, and to demonstrate that it was not a captive to business, as the administration's critics claimed (*Corporate Crime Reporter* 1988i, 12).

Conclusion

While this chapter has focused on the role of law as a means of controlling corporate violence, it is important to remember that "law is just one force among many, one vector tugging on those who labor within an organization. Its success ultimately depends upon its consistency with and reinforcement from the other factors—the organization's rules for advancement and reward, its customs, conventions, and morals" (Stone 1975, 67). Thus, the effectiveness of law is always subject to some severe constraints.

One of the principal concerns related to the legal control of corporate violence is that the legal apparatus is unresponsive to public preferences for the control of these crimes. Because of agency capture and the broad political influence of the corporate sector, the law is not accountable to the public, which ultimately bears the cost of corporate violence. The distribution of these costs is the subject of the next chapter.

Nine

Restructuring Risk Decision-Making

CORPORATE VIOLENCE sometimes occurs because of the ways in which corporations make decisions. Using cost-benefit models, corporations assess the direct and immediate impact that production decisions have upon corporate profits. For example, in order to reduce air and water pollution, companies should install pollution control equipment. However, this type of cost cuts directly into the corporation's proceeds. What the corporation would prefer is to avoid any costs whatsoever, and make pollution "someone else's" problem. Economists use the term *externalities* to refer to costs borne by third parties (the public) as a side-effect of productive activities. Thus, when a company dumps waste into a river, it is "externalizing" the cost of disposing of the wastes. Downstream residents bear the cost of this activity in the form of polluted water and illnesses caused by the pollution. When a manufacturer markets a product without adequately testing the product for safety, the costs of not testing are borne by consumers in the form of injury from unrevealed hazards associated with the product. Often, externalized costs are greater than the costs would have been if they had been internalized. For example, the costs of safety tests might have been only $250,000, but the injuries caused by the untested product cause victims and society many millions of dollars in pain and disability. To the firm, however, the economical choice is to have as many costs as possible externalized so that someone else pays part of the cost of production.

Economists define their role as identifying the most efficient distribution of externalities. When is it most efficient to require the firm to pay its own way in advance, and when is it more efficient for society as a whole that a few victims be sacrificed for the greater convenience and economy of the rest of us. Political questions are also raised by the concept of externalities, however. What social or political mechanisms are used to *decide* where the costs and benefits should fall? In addition, externalities raise ethical issues. Is there a moral responsibility to seek out and eliminate the negative externalities one creates?

A "Responsibility Model" of Externalities

Throughout this book, law has been examined as a mechanism for assigning rights and responsibilities; specifically, the right to be free of hazards and the responsibility to take precautions against hazards. Another way of looking at rights and responsibilities in relation to corporate violence is in terms of the right to make decisions regarding risks and the "responsibility" or burden of suffering risks.

Before the development of health and safety laws, decisions about health and safety were made by private individuals. Because of the decentralized character of production prior to the industrial revolution, these decisions usually had very narrow effects, creating few externalities. The shoemaker decided whether to work faster and risk hitting his thumb with the hammer. His decision affected no one but himself.

With the industrial revolution, however, the consequences of risk decisions began to extend farther and farther from decision-makers. As production and distribution were organized on a large scale, the individuals controlling these massive organizations came to possess a disproportionate amount of decision-making power regarding the risks that would be taken. These risks would be borne by customers, employees, and others. By imposing externalities in the form of exposure to risk onto others, private businessmen were able to shift some of their costs of production off themselves onto others. Moreover, the few in the corporate elite who were making the decisions were the ones most likely to benefit from the risk-taking, while those bearing the risk had little if anything to gain. By exposing *other* people to risks, businesses are in a position to benefit from the risks they create. They are able to keep production costs down, improving their overall profitability. Increased profit means increased corporate sector power, and increased wealth. The victims of corporate risk-taking, in contrast, enjoy few, if any, benefits from being exposed to these risks. While some of the risks may have offered benefits to the potential victims in the form of lower prices, higher wages, or more variety in the kinds of products available, the primary and direct benefits go to those individuals in corporations who make the decisions rather than to those bearing the risks.

Although many corporate managers are constrained by ethics and other informal controls, we have seen the enormous temptation to "externalize costs"—that is, engage in corporate violence—by exposing consumers, workers, and the public to risks of physical injury and illness. The corporation can make a bigger profit and the executive can earn a larger bonus.

Corporate violence becomes corporate crime when corporate managers make decisions about the risks they are going to expose us to, and we deem those decisions irresponsible and unreasonable. When enough political pressure is created in opposition to the risk-taking decisions of corporations, laws are passed that prohibit certain risky activities.

Looking back to history, we see that the earliest health and safety laws placed limits on the choices which could be made, but still left wide latitude for corporations to impose risks on third parties. The creation of regulatory systems further decreased the latitude open to private businessmen in their risk-taking decisions. It socialized decision-making by placing it in the hands of governmental officials rather than private individuals and by taking it away from those who would benefit from the externalization of risk.

Problems with the Socialization of Risk Decision-making

While the socialization of risk decision-making through the law is an improvement over the system of private decision-making which preceded it, this system is not without problems. A significant limitation on the effectiveness of the law is the time-lag problem. "Lawmakers have to appreciate and respond to problems that corporate engineers, chemists, and financiers were anticipating (or could have anticipated) long before—that the drugs their corporations are about to produce can alter consciousness or damage the gene pool of the human race....Even if laws could be passed to deal effectively with these dangers, until they are passed a great deal of damage—some perhaps irreversible—can be done" (Stone 1975, 94).

Because of this time-lag problem, the law will never be able to completely eliminate the power of the business sector to make decisions for the rest of us concerning the risks to which we are exposed. In fact, by depending on the law, we may be sending a signal to corporate managers that "until the law tells them otherwise, they have no responsibilities beyond the law and their impulses..." (Stone 1975, 95).

Another set of problems concerns difficulties related to the making of law. We have seen that in the absence of law, corporations and the business sector exert disproportionate power in making decisions concerning health and safety. Without law, managers make decisions about the risks that the rest of us will be exposed to. Given the strong influence of the corporate sector in the law-making process, decision-making may have been shifted to a somewhat more visible, but no more representative, forum than it was before the passage of the law. Chapter 8 discussed the problem of regulatory capture in the enforcement process. Agency capture also influences the regulations that will be passed to protect safety and health. Should a pesticide be banned as unsafe? Should drift net fishing be banned as dangerous to marine mammals? Should airbags be required in all automobiles? A captured agency, or legislators, are likely to weigh the objections of industry more heavily than the interests of the general public.

Particularly significant is the role that corporations play in the manipulation of public opinion about the law. Through advertising and information campaigns, the corporate sector shapes public opinion about health and safety problems. Chemical companies, for example, pay large amounts of money for advertising stressing the "better life" we enjoy because of new discoveries. In recent years, it has become commonplace for oil companies to advertise about the many ways in which they are "working hard" to protect the environment. These types of advertisements gloss over the potential hazards posed by these businesses and exaggerate the concern and social responsibility of the corporation. If the corporate sector possesses the power to influence public perceptions, minimizing the damage it causes and exaggerating the benefits, public decisions made by the government will reflect the preferences of corporate managers.

A final barrier to law as an answer to the problem of making decisions about risks is lack of consensus. The "public interest" is not unified on health and safety issues. As a society, we "lack consensus as to the values we want to advance" (Stone 1975, 97). Stone gives the following examples:

> Consider a drug that can benefit 99 percent of the people who suffer from some disease, but could seriously injure 1 percent: Should it be banned from the market? People value inexpensive power. They also value a clean environment. These factors point to construction of nuclear generating stations. But such stations put a risk on life.

The people who live a hundred miles from the nuclear reactor, but benefit from the cheap electricity it would generate, may favor taking some risk, especially since they are risking nothing themselves. Those who live closer to the reactor may value their safety more than the reduction in electricity costs. Each group has a different perception of the risk involved and the need to define the risk as a crime based upon their proximity to the harm (Lynch *et al.* 1988). The sorts of conflicts in public opinion can be used by the corporate sector to buttress and legitimize its own position and can lead to the paralysis of lawmakers. As a result of legislative inaction, decision-making power is once again shifted by default to the corporate sector.

The False Promise of Cost-Benefit Analysis

Given these problems in the law-making process, economists and policy analysts have advocated the use of cost-benefit analysis as a rational means of determining the optimal decision. The total social costs and the total social benefits of a proposed health or safety law are calculated. If the total social benefits exceed the total social costs, the law is economically efficient. If, however, the law would result in a net social cost, the law should not be passed. In other words, although a large number of people may be injured, the law should not prohibit a practice or product if the costs of prohibiting it are higher than the costs of the injuries.

Cost-benefit analysis is advocated as a rational solution to the problem of deciding what risks to tolerate and what risks to prohibit through the law. It appears, at least at first, to offer a neutral and non-political mechanism for making decisions about health and safety practices. Rather than allowing private corporations to make these decisions for us, rather than delegating decision-making to a highly imperfect political process through the law, we will substitute a rational decision-making process.

Unfortunately, cost-benefit analysis is not as rational and neutral as it first appears. Two principal problems arise. The first is the difficulty of attaching value to the costs and benefits which might arise. The second problem concerns the failure to consider how costs and benefits are distributed.

How Much is a Life Worth?

Most of the costs of health and safety precautions are calibrated in monetary terms. A pollution control device will cost 1.5 million dollars. A new drug that may cause birth defects costs $5 million in development and initial testing. Recalling six million automobiles will cost $60 million.

The benefits to be derived from these expenditures, however, are not usually measured in cash terms. What is the benefit of preventing one hundred cases of cancer each year? How much is it worth to spare five hundred parents the pain of giving birth to a severely deformed baby? How should we measure the benefit of avoiding several hundred serious automobile accidents caused by a faulty brake line?

While many people object to any attempt to put a dollar figure on the value of a life, economists have suggested a variety of procedures for estimating how the public really values life and health. The most common procedure is to value a life in terms of earning potential. Thus, according to calculations of the New York State Health Department in relation to Love Canal, the life of a middle-aged construction worker was worth $550,000 and the life of a school-child was worth $400,000 (Tolchin and Tolchin 1983, 129).

Another procedure for estimating the benefits of regulation is to add up the costs of compensating or treating the victims:

> The Mine Safety and Health Administration has used a value of $165,000 per life, in measuring the benefits and costs of its Respirable Coal Dust in Mines regulation. They reached this figure by simply computing the actual cost of compensating a victim of black lung disease; in other words, the money saved by preventing a case of black lung disease amounted to approximately $165,000 (Tolchin and Tolchin 1983, 129-130).

Are these realistic values? And is this a realistic means of calculating how much a human life is worth? How much does a husband or wife value their spouse? How much do children value their parents? Can these types of intimate values be turned into cash amounts? And should intimate "value" be considered when making an award?

Cost-benefit procedures, even with all their limitations, are used to estimate the value of people in all sorts of injury cases. They are even used to use estimated costs of damages payments in wrongful death suits.

Who Pays What?

Most cost-benefit analyses simply look at the aggregate social costs and benefits, without considering how these costs and benefits are distributed. Thus, all of the costs may be borne by one group of people while all of the benefits are reaped by another group. The most disadvantaged groups in society may bear the most substantial costs. That is to say, costs and benefits may be distributed unfairly, but none of these issues is taken into account by cost-benefit analysis.

A paradigmatic example of cost-benefit analysis is offered by Kip Viscusi (1984) on the costs and benefits of child-resistant medicine bottle caps. Viscusi calculates the costs of inconvenience suffered by consumers who must struggle with child-resistant caps, and concludes that the potential benefit in terms of children's lives saved is not worth it. According to Viscusi's analysis:

> CPSC-approved child-resistant caps are now designed so that an individual aged ten to forty can open the containers within five minutes. For people at the upper end of this range who open such caps once a day the total added time per year can be as much as thirty hours. If this consumer's wage rate is $10 per hour, the time cost is equivalent to a $300 annual loss. If the consumer makes choices that imply a value of his child's life of $1 million dollars, he will prefer not to use the protective caps unless they reduce the risk of death by at least 3/10,000. Even if all poisonings were fatal—and few of them are—protective caps would have to eliminate half of all poisonings for them to justify the added time costs.

Not only does Viscusi dismiss any discussion of the difference between costs to adults versus to children, he ignores significant differences in the nature of the costs compared to the nature of the benefits, putting them all on an equal monetary scale. Whether Viscusi realizes it or not, his analysis and conclusion imply that it is "worth it" to allow a few children to be poisoned to save ourselves some inconvenience, and that people, including parents, think about their children solely in cold-hearted monetary terms.

Cost-benefit analysis has been championed by the corporate sector as the appropriate criterion for making decisions regarding health and safety risks. Because of the ways in which economists have chosen to value life and health in their analyses, cost-benefit analysis has frequently offered support for corporate arguments against increased protection.

The Justice Model of Law

Despite the shortcomings of the political system as a decision-making process for assigning rights and responsibilities in relation to health and safety, there are some advantages to using the law, which should not be overlooked. One of the principal arguments for using the law in relation to health and safety problems is that justice requires a legal response. In our society, responsibility is closely connected with notions of culpability. Within this framework, someone who knowingly takes risks that may cause another injury is worthy of punishment. It is this ethical-legal principle that underlies laws dealing with reckless conduct and reckless injury. This is the principle that lead to criminal prosecutions against the Ford Motor Company, Allied Chemical, Merrell-Richardson, and Film Recovery Systems.

In addition, while punishment is deserved in its own right, it is doubly necessary in order to promote an equitable legal order. Since conventional violent crimes are among the most serious offenses, and are punished the most severely, it would be unjust to allow corporate violence to go unpunished or to be punished more leniently.

The Problem with Coercion

Although punishment is necessitated on moral grounds, policies which may be justified on moral grounds sometimes frustrate more immediate goals, such as the prevention of health and safety problems.

The law, specifically criminal and regulatory law, depends upon coercion as the means of preventing illness and injury. Coercion, however, is a most inefficient means of controlling undesirable behavior (Braithwaite 1986). The costs of surveillance alone are staggering, while the added costs of imposing coercion through the courts is also substantial.

Since resources are always scarce, enforcement officials seek ways of circumventing the inefficiency of the law. The adoption of a voluntary compliance strategy of enforcement often results. Coercion is expensive, so it is avoided even when it is appropriate.

Braithwaite (1986, 56-57) argues that coercive compliance can "sap the will of businesses to comply with the law.... Dissipating the motivation of business to strive for compliance with law is a disastrous consequence because the punitive law enforcement alternative can never fill the gaps left by the failure of persuasion and education as compliance strategies." Such a view, while appealing, may not be enough. Would education and persuasion alone be sufficient reasons for corporations to comply with the law? It would appear that this might not be the case. Since most corporate decisions are based upon cost-benefit analyses, it would be difficult for corporations to include education when making cost-benefit decisions.

Obscuring the Structural Character of Health and Safety

Finally, another drawback to the use of coercive law is that it conceptualizes health and safety problems in terms of responsibility, even when this model is inappropriate. Throughout this book, we have argued that the causes of corporate violence are best understood as a product of structural features of contemporary American society. In a sense, we are all in this mess together. Although corporate managers may have more power to make choices, their choices are constrained by the logic of modern industrial capitalism. Is it fair to impose criminal responsibility under these circumstances?

This is a particularly important issue in relation to corporate violence on the boundaries of legality. In many cases, the limits of responsibility are unclear and undefined. It may be unjust to expect corporate officials to guess what their responsibilities are. Given their conflicting responsibilities to stockholders and to the public, these decisions are not easy to make. The bus crash case discussed earlier (pp. 49-50) demonstrates the difficulties associated with distinguishing acceptable risks and criminal risks. Was the bus manufacturer producing an acceptable or criminal risk when it manufactured buses according to the existing standard even though it knew a new standard was soon to be in effect?

What would be the long-term consequences of establishing a legal precedent whereby manufacturers could be held criminally liable for failure to comply with regulations that have not yet taken effect? Questions such as these are more than just interesting discussion questions. If criminal prosecution for risk-taking becomes more common, prosecutors will have to grapple with these questions in deciding whether to charge corporations and their executives with homicide and other crimes of violence. Their answers to these questions are likely to be influenced by the law, the evidence available in a specific case, and their own subjective judgments about the blameworthiness of actors involved. In other words, do the actions and carelessness shown by the potential defendants merit the stigma of a criminal charge for murder or another violent crime?

Structure of Health and Safety

One means of remedying health and safety problems is to restructure the risk-decision system. The regulatory system has evolved as a means of doing just that. Through regulation, risk decision-making has been transferred from private corporate hands into the hands of governmental representatives. While this situation is seemingly preferable, given the fact that government employees will not directly benefit from the risks they allow, it is not at all clear that government representatives can fulfill this role in an effective and unbiased way. While the tool of cost-benefit analysis is becoming more and more common within regulatory agencies, this tool frequently distorts the value of costs and benefits.

An alternative to governmental decision-making is to restructure risk decisions so that those who bear the greatest risk have the largest choice in deciding whether or not the risk should be taken. In some areas, this kind of restructuring of decisions is already familiar. Labeling requirements and the provision of warnings give users of potentially dangerous products the information they need to decide for themselves whether they care to take the risks. A proposed FDA rule would have required that certain drugs be sold with an enclosure describing the potential side-effects of the drugs, giving consumers information needed to assess for themselves whether the benefits to them, personally, are worth the risks they are taking. A similar type of proposal was made by OSHA, which would have required employers to notify workers of all toxic chemicals employees had contact with in the work environment. Such information would have allowed workers to decide for themselves whether the compensation they were receiving for the job was sufficient to make up for the risks entailed by working with those chemicals.

Such proposals restructure decision-making about risk. Rather than choices being made by corporate managers or by government representatives, choices are made by those who would be most affected by the risks.

The feasibility and desirability of restructuring choice in this way is limited by the complexity of health and safety problems, the lack of reliable information regarding the magnitude of risks, the effects on the distribution of risk, and the difficulty of instituting the necessary changes. Because of the technical complexity of health and safety problems, many people will not be able to assimilate all of the information necessary to make informed choices. When a consumer reads the warnings on the label of an insecticide, the consumer has no basis for knowing how important it is that the precautions are followed. There is no simple way of communicating what the true magnitude of the risks might be, even if this information was known and undisputed, which it usually is not.

Such a system might find the most disadvantaged people undertaking the greatest risks, for example, working in the most risky jobs and buying riskier, but less expensive, products. The more powerless one is, in general, the more powerless one is to avoid risks. Under the current system, when serious risks are simply prohibited, the costs are more evenly distributed across socioeconomic groups.

Finally, my decision to "take a chance" and use an insecticide that poses some risk of harm to me does not protect my neighbor when I throw it way after I am through. There is little reason to presume that individuals will make more responsible choices than corporations, as long as both are operating in the same structural context.

Conclusion

While we have painted a rather gloomy picture of the prospects for controlling corporate violence, it is important to remember that great improvements have been achieved within the last twenty years. Although new hazards always appear on the horizon, some of the worst hazards of earlier years have been eliminated. In addition, the public's heightened interest in health and safety issues motivates the media to cover these issues and to give high visibility to corporate violence that is discovered. The combination of public awareness, increased litigation, and judicial activism in this area constitutes a warning to corporations and corporate officials who may be tempted to skimp on health and safety. This heightened visibility also increases the public accountability of regulatory agencies responsible for the prevention of corporate violence.

Unquestionably, some of these accomplishments have already been reversed. Disenchantment with "big government," the desire to reduce government budgets, and a resurgence of laissez-faire economic policy have undercut the ability of government agencies to fight corporate violence. These same forces have worked to reduce the amount of research that is conducted on health and safety problems, thereby reducing our information about the risks that we face. With less information being generated about health and safety problems, the public may come to the erroneous conclusion that health and safety problems have gone away. In a technological society in which science is continually inventing new machines, new chemicals, even new life forms, health and safety problems will never go away. Rather, they are a persistent feature of contemporary society.

Health and safety problems pose decisions unknown to earlier generations. Although we may object to the mechanics of cost-benefit analysis as it has been applied in relation to health and safety problems, we must also recognize that, at some level, we must make those kinds of decisions. Some risks have been found too expensive to eliminate. Some risks we decide to tolerate. The key, of course, is how those decisions are made.

Health and safety regulation has evolved into a prominent feature of modern government. Corporate violence is frightening, shocking, and disturbing. Above all, its effects extend to each and every person in our society. The law in this area is still evolving. How we view these acts will influence what the law will become. It is with this in mind that we continue to ponder: what is a crime?

Bibliography

Albanese, J.S. 1984 "Love Canal Six Years Later—The Legal Legacy." *Federal Probation* 48(June):53-58.

Altman, L.K. 1987 *Who Goes First? The Story of Self-Experimentation.* NY: Random House.

American Anti-Vivisection 1989 "Animal Experimentation is Unethical." J. Rohr (ed), *Animal Rights: Opposing Viewpoints.* San Diego: Greenhaven.

Ashford, Nicholas 1976 *Crisis in the Workplace.* Cambridge, MA: Massachusetts Institute of Technology Press.

Balkan, Sheila, Ronald J. Berger and Janet Schmidt 1980 *Crime and Deviance in America.* Belmont, CA: Wadsworth.

Baran, Paul and Paul Sweezy 1966 *Monopoly Capitalism.* NY: Modern Reader Paperbacks.

Barnett, Harold 1981 "Corporate Capitalism, Corporate Crime." *Crime and Delinquency* 27,1:4-23.

Barry, John Byrne 1991 "The Main Street Solution." *Sierra* 76,3:24-29.

Benson, Michael L. 1985 "Denying the Guilty Mind: Accounting for Involvement in a White-Collar Crime." *Criminology* 23,4:583-608.

Berg, Martin 1989 "Oil Spill Spreads to Courts; Legal Experts Split on Whether to Prosecute Exxon." *Los Angeles Daily Journal*, Vol. 102 (April 12): 1, col. 5.

Blum, R.H. 1972 *Deceivers and Deceived.* Springfield, IL: Charles Thomas.

Bolling, Richard 1986 "Money in Politics." *Annals of the American Academy of Political and Social Science* 486:76-85.

Bowles, S. and H. Gintis 1976 *Schooling in Capitalist America.* NY: Basic.

Box, Steven 1983 *Power, Crime and Mystification.* London: Tavistock.

Braithwaite, John 1982 "The Limits of Economism in Controlling Harmful Corporate Conduct." *Law and Society Review* 16(3):481-504.

Braithwaite, John 1984 *Corporate Crime in the Pharmaceutical Industry.*

Boston: Routledge and Kegan Paul.

Braithwaite, John 1985 *To Punish or Persuade: Enforcement of Coal Mine Safety.* Albany: State University of New York Press.

Braithwaite, J. and B. Fisse 1983 *The Impact of Publicity on Corporate Offenders.* Albany, NY: State University of New York Press.

Bromberg, Charles 1965 *Crime and the Mind.* NY: Macmillan.

Brown, M.H. 1980 *Laying Waste: The Poisoning of America by Toxic Chemicals.* NY: Pantheon Books.

Business Week 1985 "How Robins Will go on Paying for the Dalkon Shield." April 15, 50.

Calavita, K. 1983 "The Demise of the Occupational Safety and Health Administration: A Case Study in Symbolic Action." *Social Problems* 30(April):437-448.

Carson, W.G. 1970 "White-Collar Crime and the Enforcement of Factory Legislation." *British Journal of Criminology* 10 (October), 386.

Chambliss, William 1984 "White-Collar Crime and Criminology." *Contemporary Sociology* 13:160-162.

Chambliss, William 1975 "Toward a Political Economy of Crime." *Theory and Society* 2,2: 149-170.

Chambliss, William and Robert Seidman 1982 *Law, Order and Power.* Reading, MA: Addison-Wesley.

Claybrook, Joan 1984 *Retreat from Safety: Reagan's Attack on America's Health.* NY: Pantheon.

Clinard, M. 1983 *Corporate Ethics and Crime: The Role of Middle Management.* Beverly Hills, CA: Sage Publications.

Clinard, M. and P. Yeager 1980 *Corporate Crime.* NY: The Free Press.

Coffee, J.C., Jr. 1981 "No Soul to Damn, No Body to Kick: An Unscandalized Essay on the Problem of Corporate Punishment." *Michigan Law Review* 79, 413-24.

Coleman, James 1985 *The Criminal Elite.* NY: St. Martin's Press.

Congress of the United States 1986 *Alternatives to Animal Use in Research, Testing and Education.* Washington, D.C.: Office of Technological Assessment.

Conklin, John 1977 *Illegal But not Criminal: Business Crime in America.* Englewood Cliffs, NJ: Prentice-Hall.

Connelly, Joel 1991 "The Big Cut." *Sierra* 76,3:42-53.

Consumer Product Safety Commission 1983 *Annual Report* Washington, D.C.: U.S. Government Printing Office.

Consumer Reports 1991 *Buying Guide.* NY: Consumers Union.

Consumer Reports 1992a "Is our Fish Safe to Eat?" 57,2:103-110.

Consumer Reports 1992b "The Label Said Snapper." 57,2: 110-112.

Consumer Reports 1992c "What Else is in Fish?" 57,2: 112,114.

Consumer Reports 1992d "Fishy, Fishy: Why doesn't the U.S. Inspect More Fish?" 57,2:113.

Corporate Crime Reporter 1987a Vol. 2, No. 6 (April 23).
1987b Vol. 1, No. 5 (May 11).

1988a Vol. 2, No. 16 (April 25).
1988b Vol. 2, No. 8 (February 29).
1988c Vol. 2, No. 17 (May 2).
1988d Vol. 2, No. 4 (February 1).
1988e Vol. 2, No. 19 (May 16).
1988f Vol. 2, No. 20 (May 23).
1988g Vol. 2, No. 27 (July 11).
1988h Vol. 2, No. 25 (June 28)
1988i Vol. 2, No. 11 (March 21).

Cressey, Donald 1971 *Other People's Money: A Study in the Social-Psychology of Embezzlement.* Belmont, CA:Wadsworth.

Criminal Law and Penal Methods Reform Committee of South Australia 1977 *Fourth Report: The Substantive Criminal Law.* Adelaide: South Australian Government Printer.

Cullen, F.T., B. G. Link and C.W. Polanzi 1982 "The Seriousness of Crime Revisited: Have Attitudes Toward White-Collar Crime Changed?" *Criminology* 20:83-102.

Cullen, F.T., W.J. Maakestad, and G. Cavender 1987 *Corporate Crime Under Attack.* Cincinnati, OH: Anderson Publishing.

Cullen, F.T., W.J. Maakestad, and G. Cavender 1984 "The Ford Pinto Case and Beyond: Corporate Crime, Moral Boundaries, and the Criminal Sanction." In E. Hochstedler (ed.) *Corporations as Criminals* Beverly Hills, CA: Sage Publications.

Cullen, F., R.A. Mathers, G.A. Clark, and J.B. Cullen 1983 "Public Support for Punishing White-Collar Crime: Blaming the Victim Revisited." *Journal of Criminal Justice,* Vol. 11, 481-493.

Curren, D.J. 1984 "Symbolic Solutions to Deadly Dilemmas: An Analysis of Federal Coal Mine Health and Safety Legislation." *International Journal of Health Services* 14:5-29.

DeBonis, Jeff 1991 "The Forest Service Inside Out." *Wildlife Conservation* 94,3:10, 88-89.

DeLorean, J.Z., and J.P. Wright 1980 "A Look Inside GM." In M. Green and R. Massie, Jr. (eds.) *Big Business Reader: Essays on Corporate America* NY: Pilgrim Press.

Department of Labor 1986 *Annual Report of the Secretary of Labor Under the Federal Mine Safety and Health Act of 1977, FY 86.* Washington, D.C.: U.S. Government Printing Office.

Domhoff, G.W. 1979 *The Powers That Be: Processes of Ruling Class Domination in America.* NY: Vintage Books.

Donnelly, Patrick 1982 "The Origins of the Occupational Safety and Health Act of 1970." *Social Problems* 30:13-25.

Dowie, M. 1977 "Pinto Madness." *Mother Jones Magazine* (Sept-Oct), 18-24, 28-32.

Dowie, M. 1982 "The Illusion of Safety." *Mother Jones Magazine* (June), 36-48.

Epstein, Samuel 1979 *The Politics of Cancer.* NY:Anchor.

Ermann, M.D. and W.H. Clements, Jr. 1984 "The Interfaith Center on Corporate Responsibility and its Campaign Against Marketing Infant Formula in the Third World." *Social Problems*, 32, 185-196.

Ermann, M.D. and R.J. Lundman 1987 *Corporate and Governmental Deviance— Problems of Organizational Behavior in Contemporary Society*, Third Edition. NY: Oxford University Press.

F.D.A. Drug Review 1990 "Post-Approval Risks." 1976-1985. Washington, D.C.: U.S. General Accounting Office.

Finney, Henry C. and Henry R. Lesieur 1982 "A Contingency Theory of Organizational Crime." *Research in the Sociology of Organizations* 1, 255-299.

Fisse, B. 1981 "Community Service as a Sanction Against Corporations." *Wisconsin Law Review* 1981, 970-1017.

Fisse, B. and J. Braithwaite 1983 *The Impact of Publicity on Corporate Offenders*. Albany, NY: State University of New York Press.

Fisse, B. and J. Braithwaite 1984 "Sanctions Against Corporations: Dissolving the Monopoly of Fines." In *Business Regulation in Australia*, ed. Roman Tomasic. Sydney: CCH.

Frank, Nancy 1988 "Unintended Murder and Corporate Risk-Taking: Defining the Concept of Justifiability." *Journal of Criminal Justice* 16(1):17-24.

Frank, N. 1983 "From Criminal to Civil Penalties in the History of Health and Safety Law." *Social Problems* (July), 532-544.

Frank, N. and M. Lombness 1988 *Controlling Corporate Illegality: The Regulatory Justice System*. Cincinnati, OH: Anderson.

Friedman, M. 1962 *Capitalism and Freedom*. Chicago: University of Chicago Press.

Gibson, R. 1985 "Illegal Aliens Picked for Cyanide Work, Bookkeeper Testifies." *Chicago Tribune*, April 24, 1985.

Geis, Gilbert 1978 "Deterring Corporate Crime." In M.D. Erman and R.L. Lundmas (eds) *Corporate and Governmental Deviance*. NY: Oxford.

Goldberg, A. M. and J. M. Frazier 1989 "Alternatives to Animals in Toxicity Testing." *Scientific American* 261:24-30.

Goodall, Jane 1989 "Primate Research is Inhumane." In J. Rohr (ed), *Animal Rights: Opposing Viewpoints*. San Diego: Greenhaven.

Gordon, David 1971 "Class and the Economics of Crime." *The Review of Radical Political Economy* 3,3:51-72.

Green, Mark 1972 *The Closed Enterprise System*. NY:Grossman.

Green, Mark and Robert Massie, Jr. 1980 *The Big Business Reader: Essays on Corporate America*. NY: Pilgrim Press.

Groveman, B. and J. Segal 1985 "Pollution Police Pursue Chemical Criminals." *Business and Society Review* (Fall):39-42.

Groves, W. Byron and Michael J. Lynch 1990 "Reconciling Structural and Subjective Approaches to the Study of Crime." *Journal of Research in Crime and Delinquency* 27,4:348-375.

Groves, W. Byron and Nancy Frank 1987 "Punishment, Privilege and the

Sociology of Structured Choice." In W. B. Groves and G.R. Newman (eds.) *Punishment and Privilege*. NY: Harrow and Heston.

Groves, W. Byron and Robert J. Sampson 1987 "Traditional Contributions to Radical Criminology." *Journal of Research in Crime and Delinquency* 24,3:181-214.

Hans, V.P. and M.D. Ermann 1989 "Responses to Corporate Versus Individual Wrongdoing." *Law and Human Behavior* 13(2), 151-165.

Health and Humane Research 1991 *Annual Report*. Jenkintown, PA: American Antivivisection Society.

Henry, Jules 1965 *Culture Against Man*. NY: Vintage.

Hill, S.L. 1987 *Corporate Violence—Injury and Death for Profit*. Totowa, NJ: Roman and Littlefield.

Hinds, M. 1982 "Products Unsafe at Home are Still Unloaded Abroad." *New York Times*, August 22, E9.

Hirschi, T. 1969 *The Causes of Delinquency*. Berkeley: University of California Press.

Hirschi, T. and M.Gottfredson 1987 "Causes of White-Collar Crime." *Criminology* 25:949-974.

Hochstedler, Ellen 1984 *Corporations as Criminals*. Beverly Hills: Sage Publications.

Hohenemser, Christopher, Roger Kasperson and Robert W. Kates 1980 "A Structural Model of Technological Hazard." Paper presented at the annual meetings of the American Society of Toxicology, Washington, D.C.

Jackall, Robert 1988 *Moral Mazes*. New York: Oxford University Press

Jeffrey, C. Ray 1990 *Criminology: An Interdisciplinary Approach*. Englewood Cliffs, NJ: Prentice Hall.

Josephson, Matthew 1934 *The Robber Barons: The Great American Capitalists, 1861-1901*. NY: Harcourt, Brace and Company.

Kadish, S. 1963 "Some Observations on the Use of Criminal Sanctions in Enforcing Economic Regulations." *University of Chicago Law Review* , 30: 423.

Kallet, Arthur and F.J. Schlink 1933 *100,000,000 Guinea Pigs: Dangers in Everyday Foods, Drugs and Cosmetics*. NY: Grosset and Dunlap.

Katz, Jack 1988 *The Seductions of Crime*. NY: Basic.

Katz, Jack 1980 "The Social Movement Against White-Collar Crime." In E. Bittner and S. Messinger (eds.) *Criminology Review Yearbook*. Volume 2. Beverly Hills: Sage.

Kaufman, Stephen 1989 "Most Animal Experimentation does not Benefit Human Health." In J. Rohr (ed.) *Animal Rights: Opposing Viewpoints*. San Diego: Greenhaven.

Kaufman, S.R., and Betsy Todd 1989 *Perspectives on Animal Research*. Volume 1. NY: Medical Research Modernization Committee.

Kelley, C. Brian 1981 "Kepone." In R Nader, R Brownstein, and J. Richard (eds.) *Who's Poisoning America: Corporate Polluters and Their Victims in the Chemical Age*.

Kleinfield, N.R. 1985 "Workers Suffer When Scandal Strikes Company." *The Milwaukee Journal* July 14, 1985, Business Section, 1, 5.

Kolko, G. 1963 *The Triumph of Conservatism.* Glencoe, IL: Free Press.

Kramer, R. 1984 "Corporate Criminality: The Development of an Idea." In E. Hochstedler (ed.) *Corporations as Criminals.* Beverly Hills: Sage.

Kuruc, M. 1985 "Putting Polluters in Jail—the Imposition of Criminal Sanctions on Corporate Defendants Under Environmental Statutes." *Land and Water Review* 20:93-108.

Luoma, Jon R. 1991 "The Unfriendly Skies." *Wildlife Conservation* 94,3:70-83.

Lynch, M.J. 1990 "The Greening of Criminology: A Perspective on the 1990s." *The Critical Criminologist* 2,3:3-4, 11-12.

Lynch, M. J. and W. B. Groves 1989 *Primer in Radical Criminology.* NY: Harrow and Heston.

Lynch, M.J., M. K. Nalla, and K. Miller 1989 "Cross-Cultural Perceptions of Deviance: The Case of Bhopal." *Journal of Research in Crime and Delinquency* 26,1:7-35.

Lynxwiler, J., N. Shover, and D. Clelland 1983 "The Organization of Inspector Discretion in a Regulatory Bureaucracy." *Social Problems* 30(April):425-435.

Lynxwiler, J., N. Shover, and D. Clelland 1984 "Determinants of Sanction Severity in a Regulatory Bureaucracy," in Ellen Hochstedler (ed.) *Corporations as Criminals,* Newbury Park, CA: Sage Publications.

Maakestad, W.J. 1983 "*State v. Ford Motor Co.*: Constitutional, Libertarian, and Moral Perspectives." *Saint Louis University Law Journal,* 27, 857-880.

Magnuson, J.C. and G.C. Leviton 1987 "Policy Considerations in Corporate Criminal Prosecutions After *People v. Film Recovery Systems, Inc.*" *Notre Dame Law Review* 62(5), 913-939

Mardon, Mark 1991 "Maneuvers in the Teak Wars." *Sierra* 76,3:30,32-33,36.

Margulies, L. 1980 "Babies, Bottles, and Breast Milk: The Nestles Syndrome." In M. Green and R. Massie, Jr. (eds.) *Big Business Reader: Essays on Corporate America,* NY: Basic Books.

Marx, Karl 1977[1868] *Capital,* Volume I. NY: International.

Marx, Karl and Fredrick Engels 1970[1846] *The German Ideology.* NY: International.

Mathias, Charles 1986 "Should there be Financing of Congressional Campaigns?" Annals of the Academy of Political and Social Science 486:64-75.

Merton, Robert 1938 "Social Structure and Anomie." *American Sociological Review* 3:672-682.

Messerschmidt, J. 1986 *Capitalism, Patriarchy and Crime.* Totowa, N.J.: Roman and Littlefield.

Michalowski, R.J. 1985 *Order, Law and Crime: An Introduction to Criminology.* NY: Random House.

Michalowski, R.J. and R. Kramer 1987 "The Space Between the Laws: The Problem of Corporate Crime in Transnational Context." *Social Problems* 34(February):34-53.

Mills, C.W. 1958 *The Sociological Imagination.* NY: Oxford.

Mills, C.W. 1956 *The Power Elite.* NY: Oxford University Press.

Mintz, M. 1989 "A Snail's Pace on Pacemakers." *The Washington Post: National Weekly Edition* 6(43), August 28-September 3, 33-34.

Monahan, J., R.W. Novaco and G. Geis 1979 "Corporate Violence: Research Strategies for Community Psychology." In D. Adelson and T. Sarbin (eds)*Challenges for the Criminal Justice System.* NY: Human Sciences Press.

Mueller, G.O.W. 1979 "Offenses Against the Environment and their Prevention: An International Appraisal." *Annals of the American Academy of Political and Social Science* 444:56-66.

Murphy, W.M. 1983 "Enforcing Environmental Laws—A Modern Day Challenge." *FBI Law Enforcement Bulletin* 52(November):15-19.

Nadel, Mark 1971 *The Politics of Consumer Protection.* Indianapolis: Bobbs-Merrill.

Nader, Ralph 1965 *Unsafe at Any Speed: The Designed in Dangers of the American Automobile.* NY: Grossman.

Nalla, Mahesh and Graeme R. Newman 1990 *A Primer in Private Security.* NY: Harrow and Heston.

Nelson, D. 1985 "Foul Haze Veiled Factory Death." *The Daily Herald*, Palatine Inverness Edition. April 16, 1,3.

New York Times 1984 April 10, p. A22.

Newman, D. J. 1957 "Public Attitudes Toward a Form of White Collar Crime." *Social Problems* 23:228-232.

Newsweek 1981 "Pesticides' Global Fallout." August 17, 53-55.

Owens, P. 1985 "Death of worker Puts Factory Safety on Trial." *Newsday.* June 6, 1, 31.

Pacheco, Alex 1991 "Newsletter" People for the Ethical Treatment of Animals.

Page, Joseph and Mary-Win O'Brien 1973 *Bitter Wages.* NY: Grossman.

Passas, Nikos 1990 "Anomie and Corporate Deviance." *Contemporary Crises* 14,157-178.

Pearce, Frank 1976 *Crimes of the Powerful.* London: Pluto Press.

Postrel, Virginia 1990 "Forget Left and Right, the Politics of the Future will be Growth versus Green." *UTNE Reader* 40:57-58.

Quinney, Richard 1980 *Class, State and Crime.* NY: Longman.

Quirk, P.J. 1981 *Industry and Influence in Federal Regulatory Agencies.* Princeton: Princeton University Press.

Quirk, P.J. 1980 "Food and Drug Administration." In J.Q. Wilson (ed.) *The Politics of Regulation.* NY: Basic Books.

Rabinovitch, John David 1981 "The Politics of Poison." In R. Nader, R. Brownstein, and J. Richard (eds), *Who's Poisoning America: Corporate Polluters and Their Victims in the Chemical Age.*

Rainforest Action Network 1990a "Hawaiian Tropical Forest Alert." Newlestter.

Rainforest Action Network 1990b "Japan: #1 Importer of Tropical Timber." Newsletter. October 20-28.

Rainforest Action Network 1990c "Avoid Japan Bashing." Newsletter. October 20-28.

Rainforest Action Network 1990d "Tropical Timber Factsheet." 301 Broadway, Suite A, S.F., CA, 94133.

Rainforest Action Network 1990e "Logging and the Indigenous Peoples of Malaysia." Factsheet. 301 Broadway, Suite A, S.F., CA, 94133.

Rauber, Paul 1991 "Losing the Initiative?" *Sierra* 76,3: 20-24.

Reckless, Walter 1973 *The Crime Problem.* NY: Appleton-Century.

Reiman, J. 1990 *The Rich Get Richer and The Poor Get Prison.* Third Edition. NY: Wiley.

Ross, E.A. 1907 *Sin and Society.* Boston: Houghton, Mifflin.

Ross, E.A. 1907[1977] "The Criminaloid." In G. Geis and R. Meier (eds.) *White Collar Crime.* NY: The Free Press.

Salmon, Carol-Linnea 1989 "Milking Deadly Dollars from the Third World" *Business and Society Review* 68 (Winter): 43-48.

Sale, K. 1990 "The Environmental Crisis is not Our Fault." *UTNE Reader* 40:53-54.

Salsburg, D.S. 1983 "The Lifetime Feeding Study in Mice and Rats—An Examination of its Validity as a Bioassay for Human Carcinogens." *Fundamental and Applied Toxicology* 3:63-67.

Scanlan, Christopher 1991a "U.S. Ships Toxic Goods to the World." *Tallahassee Democrat* May 19:1a, 5a.

Scanlan, Christopher 1991b "The Toxic Trade will likely keep Churning." *Tallahassee Democrat* May 19:5a.

Scarpitti, F.R. and A.A. Block 1987 "America's Toxic Waste Racket—Dimensions of the Environmental Crisis." In Tim Bynum (ed.) *Organized Crime in America.* Monsey, NY: Criminal Justice Press.

Schwendinger, Herman and Julia Schwendinger 1970 "Defenders of Order or Guardians of Human Rights?" *Issues in Criminology* 5:113-146.

Seigel, S. 1989 "Animal Testing is Unnecessary and Dangerous to Human Health." *UTNE Reader* 39:47-49.

Shapiro, S. 1984 *Wayward Capitalists.* New Haven: Yale University Press.

Sharpe, R., 1988 *The Cruel Deception: The Use of Animals in Medical Research.* Wellingsborough:Thorsons.

Shover, N., D.A. Clelland and J. Lynxwiler 1986 *Enforcement and Negotiation: Constructing a Regulatory Bureaucracy.* Albany, NY: State University of New York Press.

Silver, George 1976 "The Medical Insurance Disease." *The Nation* 222,12.

Silverman, Milton and Philip R. Lee 1974 *Pills, Profits, and Politics.* Berkeley: University of California Press.

Silverman, Milton, Phillip Lee, and Mia Lydecker 1982 *Prescription for Death: The Drugging of the Third World.* Berkeley: University of California Press.

Simon, D.R. and D. S. Eitzen 1990 *Elite Deviance.* Boston: Simon and Schuster.

Sinclair, U. 1951 *The Jungle.* NY: Harper and Brothers.

Soloman, L.D. and N.S. Nowak 1980 "Managerial Restructuring: Prospects for a New Regulatory Tool." *Notre Dame Lawyer* 56, 120-40.

Spurgeon W.A. and T.P. Fagan 1981 "Criminal Liability for Life-Endangering Corporate Conduct." *Journal of Criminal Law and Criminology* 72(Summer):381-630.

Stone, C. 1975 *Where the Law Ends: The Social Control of Corporate Behavior.* NY: Harper Colophon Books.

Stone, C. 1982 "A Slap on the Wrist for the Kepone Mob." In *Corporate and Governmental Deviance: Problems of Organizational Behavior in Modern Society,* 2nd edition, NY: Oxford University Press.

Strobel, L.P. 1980 *Reckless Homicide? Ford's Pinto Trial.* South Bend, IN: And Books.

Sutherland, E.H. 1983 *White Collar Crime: The Uncut Version.* New Haven, CT: Yale University Press.

Sutherland, E. H. 1949 *White-Collar Crime.* NY: Holt, Reinhart and Winston.

Sutherland, E.H. 1945 "Is 'White-Collar Crime' Crime?" *American Sociological Review* 10:132-139.

Sutherland, E. H. 1941 "Crime and Business." *Annals of the American Society of Political and Social Science* 217:

Sutherland, E.H. 1940 "White-Collar Criminality." *American Sociological Review* 5:1-12.

Stroman, D.F. 1979 *The Quick Knife: Unnecessary Surgery in the USA.* Port Washington, NY: Kennikat Press.

Swanson, W. and G. Schultz 1982 *Prime Rip.* Englewood Cliffs, NJ: Prentice Hall.

Swartz, J. 1975 "Silent Killers at Work." *Crime and Social Justice* 10:15-20.

Sykes, G. and D. Matza 1957 "Techniques of Neutralization: A Theory of Delinquency." *American Sociological Review* 22, 664-670.

Szasz, A. 1984 "Industrial Resistance to Occupational Safety and Health Legislation: 1971-1981." *Social Problems* 32:103-116.

Szasz, A. 1986 "Corporations, Organized Crime, and the Disposal of Hazardous Waste: An Examination of the Making of A Criminogenic Regulatory Structure." *Criminology* 24:1-27.

Time 1989 "Joe's Bad Trip." July 24.

Tolchin, Susan J. and Martin Tolchin 1983 *Dismantling America: The Rush to Deregulate.* Boston: Houghton Mifflin.

UTNE Reader 1990 (See various articles on the Green Movement). Volume 40.

Vandivier, K. 1982 "Why Should My Conscience Bother Me?" In M.D. Ermann and R.J. Lundman (eds.) *Corporate Crime and Governmental Deviance: Problems of Organizational Behavior in Contemporary Society,* 2nd edition. NY: Oxford University Press.

Vaughn, E. 1982 "Toward Understanding Unlawful Organizational Behavior." *Michigan Law Review* 80,7:1377-1402.

Veblen, Thorstein 1899[1953] *The Theory of the Leisure Class.* NY: Mentor.

Viscusi, W. Kip 1984 *Regulating Consumer Product Safety.* Washington, D.C.: American Enterprise Institute for Public Policy Research.

Walijassper, Jay 1990 "Who are the Greens and What do They Believe?" *UTNE Reader* 40:58-60.

Weir, D. 1987 *The Bhopal Syndrome.* San Francisco: Center for Investigative Reporting.

Weir, D. and M. Shapiro 1982 *Circle of Poison.* San Francisco: Institute for Food and Development Policy.

Wilson, J.Q. 1980 *The Politics of Regulation.* NY: Basic Books.

Yale Law Journal 1979 "Structural Crime and Institutional Rehabilitation: A New Approach to Corporate Sentencing." *Yale Law Journal* 89, 353-75.

Yoder, S.A. 1978 "Criminal Sanctions for Corporate Illegality." *Journal of Criminal Law and Criminology* 69: 40-58.

Yohay, S.C. and G.E. Dodge 1987 "Criminal Prosecutions for Occupational Injuries: An Issue of Growing Concern." *Employee Relations Law Journal* 13(Autumn):197-223.

Zwick, David and Mary Benstock 1971 *Water Wasteland.* Washington, D.C.: Center for the Study of Responsive Law.

Index